Francisco Bruquetas

ADVANCED
SPANISH

USING ENGLISH TO LEARN SPANISH

ADVANCED SPANISH: USING ENGLISH TO LEARN SPANISH
© 2012 Francisco de la Calle

ISBN 978-0-578-10435-5

R150308

Editorial Assistant: Vanessa Sofia Goulart

Cover Art: Francisco de la Calle

Bruquetas Publishing
88 S. Third St. #162, San José, California 95112, USA
www.BruquetasPublishing.com

For Michelle

The Book at a Glance

Table of Contents

INTRODUCTION
INTRODUCCIÓN

Advanced Spanish is intended for English speakers who can already communicate in Spanish, and want to go to the next level of speaking fluently and properly.

This book presents topics that are traditionally more foreign to the English speaker but with a different approach: so that they can give them a new try. Its methodology, *Using English to Learn Spanish,* takes advantage of the similarities between the two languages. The book displays the translation of all examples for the readers to do their own associations; and it explains the basic grammar concepts for the readers to understand the structural commonalities of the two languages. This book includes a glossary of grammatical terms as an appendix for easy reference.

The selection of topics of advanced Spanish is the following:

> *Chapter 1 Pronunciation*
> *Chapter 2 Orthography*
> *Chapter 3 Adjectives*
> *Chapter 4 Pronouns*
> *Chapter 5 Prepositions*
> *Chapter 6 Subjunctive*
> *Chapter 7 Other Considerations on Verbs*
> *Chapter 8 How to Learn Words Efficiently*

Chapter 7 Other Considerations on Verbs, focuses on the differences between the infinitive and gerund forms (to sing vs. singing), between the preterite and the imperfect past (I sang vs. I used to sing), and between the verbs "ser" and "estar" (= to be).

Chapter 8 How to Learn Words Efficiently provides a set of recommendations on continuous education because, even after speaking a language proficiently, you never stop learning new words. Part of the method used includes learning words from your areas of interest, words that should make your learning process fun, and continuous.

Also, as the other books from the series, *Advanced Spanish* tries to maintain the natural order of the language: Sounds, Vocabulary and Grammar.

SOUNDS:	letters
VOCABULARY:	words
GRAMMAR:	sentences

However, the reader is who must judge the level of depth that must delve into when reading this book, since all speakers are different and have had a different language acquisition history.

Each chapter displays:

- **The core of the lesson**, with: language patterns, examples, and golden rules

- **Frequently Asked Questions**

- **Exercises**

The book uses a standard Spanish: the recommended pronunciation, vocabulary and grammar follows the norms of the *New Grammar of the Spanish Language* (*Nueva Gramática de la Lengua Española*) 2010. This book is a joint effort of the *Real Academia Española* and the *Asociación de Academias de la Lengua Española*, which represent the 22 countries that speak Spanish in the world, including the U.S., Puerto Rico, and the Philippines.

Spanish is a very unified language, nevertheless for the students to have a better understanding of what the dialectal differences are, this book includes as an appendix a summary of the characteristics of the three major normative dialects, those of Spain, Argentina and the rest of Latin America.

Without further ado, here is Advanced Spanish.

1. PRONUNCIATION
PRONUNCIACIÓN

When reviewing your Spanish, pronunciation should be the first step, since sounds (letters) are the elemental bricks of language building.

Keep in mind that Spanish individual sound-values don't necessarily coincide with the English counterparts. For example, the last letter in: total (Sp.)/total (Eng.), or col (Sp.)/ call(Eng.) would be recognized as an "L" by both Spanish and English speakers, however they will pronounce this sound differently.

Differences like this make the learner have an accent in Spanish. But those adjustments to the new language occur fast (and for the most part unconsciously) when trying to imitate the native speakers. English has a much wider range of sounds than Spanish, which gives English speakers an advantage as learners.

However many students with an advanced level have knowledge gaps in a more fundamental stage: that of simple sound-values. This chapter will present the sound-values, focusing on letters that are commonly unrecognizably pronounced, and those sounds that are commonly unrecognizably written. Examples of those mistakes are pronouncing the word "hola" as /hola/ instead of /ola/, or /pingüino/ (= penguin) as "pinguino" instead of "pingüino."

Vowels

Unlike English, the sound-value of the Spanish vowels doesn't change. Thus, for example, the letter "a" is always pronounced in the same way. In English "a" sounds different in *apple* than in *cable*.

The following table shows the sound-value of the vowels by comparing them with their English counterparts.

Letter	Sound	Example in Spanish
a	As the "a" in "father"	Argentina
e	As the "e" in "bed"	emperador (= emperor)
i	As the "ea" in "meat"	Italia (= Italy)
o	As the "o" in "open"	oferta (= offer)
u	As the "oo" in "boot"	iluminación (= illumination)

Remember that they don't sound identical in both languages, but they are close enough. For example, the English "oo" of "good" is slightly longer than the Spanish "u."

In addition, the letter "y" sounds the same as a Spanish "i" when at the end of a word, as in "soy" (= I am), or as in the word "y" (= and).

The letter "u" is silent in the combinations "gue," "gui," "que," "qui,", e.g. "guerra" (= war), "guitarra" (= guitar), "queso" (= cheese), "Quito." In English, it happens the same in words as "guest," "guitar," "Quito," "antique."

Certain combinations of vowel sounds also become problematic since they don't appear in English with the same sound-value. This is the case of EU, UO, EA, EE, in words as: "reunión" (= meeting), "búho" (= owl) or "leer" (= to read).

Consonants

The consonants are those letters (sounds) that are not vowels. They are:

Letter	Sound	Examples in Spanish
b	As in English.	Bolivia
c	**Two possible sounds:** When followed by *a, o, u* (ca, co, cu) or by a consonant (cr, cl) it sounds as the hard "c" in English. Otherwise, it sounds as the "c" in "**c**ement." Only in Spain, it sounds as the "th" in "**th**ing,"	→ capital, coma, curioso, crema, clase (= capital, comma, curious, cream, class) → cemento, cine (= cement, cinema)
d	Weaker than in English.	Diamante (= diamond)
f	As in English.	Filipinas (= Philippines)
g	**Two possible sounds:** 1. As the guttural "g" in English, when followed by *a, o, u* (ga, go, gu, gue, gui) or a consonant (gl, gr) 2. Otherwise (ge ,gi), it sounds as the "h" in "**H**elen, **h**ippo."	→ gato, golf, gurú, **gu**errilla, **gu**itarra, globo, gris (= cat, golf, guru, guerilla, guitar, balloon, gray) → general, gigante (= general, giant)
h	Silent unless combined in "ch."	hora (= hour)
j	As the English "h" in "**h**am, **H**elen, **h**ippo or **h**ome."	San José
k	As in English.	kilogramo (= kilogram)
l	As in English.	lámpara (= lamp)
m	As in English.	médico (= doctor)
n	As in English.	Nicaragua
ñ	Like the "gn" of "cognac."	coñac (= cognac)
p	As in English.	Perú
q	As in English (In Spanish, q is always followed by u).	Quito

Letter	Sound	Examples in Spanish
r	**Two possible sounds:** 1. As the English "r," if not at the beginning of the word. 2. Or, at the beginning of a word, or paired, it sounds stronger.	→ hora (= hour) → rápido, carro (= rapid, car)
s	As in English.	sonido (= sound)
t	As in English.	Tijuana
v	As the English "b."	Venezuela
w	As in English.	waterpolo (= waterpolo)
x	As in English.	examen (= exam)
y	**Two possible sounds.** 1. It sounds like "ea" of "meal," when either at the end of words or isolated (meaning "and") **2.** Otherwise, it sounds as the English "j" in "major."	→ y (= and), Uruguay → mayor (= major)
z	As the "c" in "cement." Only in Spain it is as the English "th."	zoo (= zoo)

Remember:

Letters b and **v** both sound like English "b."

Letter c has two sounds. In "**ce**," "**ci**," letter "c" sounds like in English. Only in Spain, it sounds as the th of **thunder**. Otherwise, in "**ca**," "**co**," "**cu**," "**cr**," "**cl**," it sounds like in English (like a "k").

Letter d is weaker than that of English. In Spanish "d" sounds especially weak when it's placed between vowels. Thus the words "cansado" (= tired) is pronounced "cansao" by some speakers.

Letter g has two sounds (as it does in English). In "**ga**," "**go**," "**gu**," it sounds as the g in the English **garage**, **government**, **guru**. Also as in English, the combination **"gue"**, **"gui"** will sound: guerilla and guitar. This very sound is the one for the combinations gl, gr, like in gland, grand. However ge, gi sound like the Spanish "j" of "San José," which is a stronger than the English "h" of "ham."

Letter h is silent. However **"ch"** is pronounced like English of "China."

Letter ñ doesn't exist in English as a letter. However the sound is in popular words like "piñata," "jalapeño" or "El Niño" (the atmospheric phenomenon). It sounds like the gn in cognac or filet mignon (close to the "nj" in injection).

Letter q can only be found in the combination with "u" to form: **"que,"** **"qui."** sounding as "k." Thus, the two spellings kilo and quilo result in the same pronunciation.

Letter r has two pronunciations: weak and strong "r" (simple and multiple vibrating r). The weak sound corresponds to that of the English "r." The strong r is represented either by the single letter r when in the beginning of the word or by **"rr."** English doesn't have this sound. The strong r sound has the same articulation as the weak "r" but the tongue vibrates (close to the onomatopoeia "brrr" or "grrr").

Letter y has two sounds. One as the Spanish vowel "i," (the English "ea" of meal") when meaning "and," or when at the end of a word, like "Paraguay." Otherwise it sounds as the English "j" in joke.

Letter z sounds as the "c" of "ceremony". Only in Spain, it sounds as the "th" of **th**under.

In addition, "**ch, ll, rr**" have one single sound each:

Pair	Sound	Examples in Spanish
ch	As in English.	Chile
ll	As the English "j" in joke.	llama (= flame)
rr	As the English "r," but it vibrates multiple times.	carro (= car)

Remember that in Spanish you may find cc, mb, mp, etc., but each letter of the pair belongs to different syllable. E.g. **ac-t**or, **ac-c**ión, a-dic-to, e-le-fan-te (= actor, action, addict, elephant)

Frequently Asked Questions

FAQ 1: Why in my dictionary are "CH" and "LL" considered single letters?

Considering "CH" and "LL" as single letters is an **old** rule not in use any more.

In old dictionaries letter "CH" is placed after letter "C," and "LL" is placed after letter "L."

FAQ 2: Is the letter "y" a vowel?

Vowel is defined as a type of letter or as a type of sound. The letters a, e, i, o and u always have vowel sounds. The letter "y" may sound as a vowel in certain cases.

In Spanish, the letter "y" sounds the same as the Spanish letter "i" when it means "and" (Fernando y Carlos = Fernando and Carlos); or when at the end of the word, e.g. hay (= there is), ley (= law), voy (= I go).

In those cases, letter "y" is considered as a vowel. Otherwise "y" is a consonant as the English "j" in "jam."

FAQ 3: Should "y" and "ll" sound the same? Why do some people use an "i?"

Originally "ll" sounded as the English "ll" in "million" (It still sounds this way in some places of Spain and Bolivia). With time, "ll" acquired the sound of the "y." **Nowadays** both "y" and "ll" sound the same. On the other hand, there are variations in the way Spanish speakers pronounce "y." In Argentina, both sound especially strong (See *Appendix A: Notes About Dialects*).

The sound for the Spanish "y" lends itself to move to other sounds. One is the Spanish ll, as explained above, others are the "i," and the English "sh" (the latter is common in Argentina) this is why you can hear "calle" as: /kalie/, /kaye/, /kaie/, /kashe/.

This variation can look very foreign for an English speaker, but English also offers similar variations. For example, the letter "t" , other that its normative sound as a "t" (in "time" /taim/) or a "sh" (in "perfection" /perfekshon/), it admits the sounds "ch" (in "future" /fiuchur/), or "r" (in "greater" /greirer/) or even silent (in "twenty" /tueni/).

FAQ 4: What are the two dots on the "u" in "lingüista?"

Words like "lingüista" or "pingüino" (= linguist, penguin) have this symbol
called dieresis (diéresis, in Spanish). As we saw, the "u" is silent in the
combination "gue," "gui." To spell a word where the "u" needs to sound, you
need dieresis. It is also used in English by some newspapers to mark that a
certain letter must be pronounced, like "coöperation" (otherwise, "oo" would
sound like in "boot"). Spanish uses this symbol with the same intent: to mark
that "u" must be pronounced.

FAQ 5: I've seen both "México" and "Méjico." What's the right spelling?

Both. The Spanish words México, Nuevo México, Texas and Oaxaca can be
spelled with "x" or with "j." The **Mexican** Academy of Spanish Language
decided to spell it with "x" for historical reasons, although, in any case, it is
pronounced with a Spanish "j" sound. In the rest of the Spanish speaking
countries, these words are spelled with "j" (Méjico, Nuevo Méjico, Tejas,
Oajaca and a few others).

FAQ 6: Why have I never heard the English "th" sound in Spanish?

Using the "s" sound instead of "th" sound is also accepted. This use is found in
Latin America, including Mexico and the US (See *Appendix A: Notes About
Dialects*).

**FAQ 7: Sometimes native speakers don't pronounce the "d" or the "s." Is
there any rule for it?**

Still in a normative Spanish "d" sounds weak when is placed between vowels
or at the end of a syllable.

$$de\text{-}do^* \quad \rightarrow \quad /de\delta o/^{**} \quad (= dedo)$$
$$can\text{-}sa\text{-}da \quad \rightarrow \quad /kansa\delta a/ \quad (= tired)$$
$$so\text{-}le\text{-}dad \quad \rightarrow \quad /soleda\delta/ \quad (= solitude)$$

(*) Underline indicates stress
(**) δ represents the weak d

However, in some non-normative dialects (as in some parts of southern Spain
and coastal areas of Latin America), the weak "d" tends to be silent.

de-do   → /d<u>e</u>o/   (= dedo)
can-sa-da → /kans<u>a</u>/ (= tired)
so-le-dad → /soled<u>a</u>/ (= solitude)

In the same way, also in those non-normative dialects, the "s," tend to be silent.

no-so-tros → /nos<u>o</u>tro/ or /no<u>o</u>tro/ (= we)
casas   → /k<u>a</u>sa/   (= house)

As a general tendency in Spanish, a consonant in the beginning of a syllable (the explosive part of the syllable) sounds much stronger than that at the end of it.

sol (= sun) [strong s, weak l], it can become "so"
los (= the) [strong l, weak s], it can become "lo"

Spanish speakers learning English tend to underestimate the importance of verbal endings:

"~~I have work there.~~" instead of "I have work**ed** there."
"~~He work there.~~"   instead of   "He work**s** there."

Exercises

Exercise 1.

Write a phonetic transcription of the 30 words below. For this exercise use the following capital letters:

- [A] for the English "a" in "father" (the Spanish "a") *
- [E] for the English "e" in "bed" (the Spanish "e")
- [I] for the English "ea" in "meat" (the Spanish "i")
- [O] for the English "o" in "open" (the Spanish "o")
- [U] for the English "oo" in "boot" (the Spanish "u")
- [H] for the English "h" in "ham" (the Spanish "j")
- [G] for the English "g" in "girl" (the Spanish "g" in "gas")
- [Y] for the English "g" in "gel" (the Spanish "y" in "yema")
- [RR] for the Spanish "rr"

Use the corresponding lower case letter for the rest of the sounds. Also use the underscore to mark the stress.

For example: the word "vaca" (= cow) would be: /bAkA/

The reason for using different symbols is to remind you that those letters don't have the same sound-value in both languages.

#	Spanish	English	Answer
1.	murciélago	bat (animal)	mUrsIEIAgO
2.	bravo	courageous	brAbO
3.	cohete	rocket	kOEtE
4.	cajón	drawer	kAHOn
5.	cereza	cherry	sErEsA
6.	cima	top of a hill	sImA
7.	comarca	region	kOmArkA
8.	cuña	wedge	kUñA
9.	alambique	still	AlAmbIkE
10.	quilla	keel	kIYa
11.	zirconita	zircon	sIrkonItA
12.	cazo	pan	kAsO
13.	zueco	sabot	sUEkO
14.	cazuela	casserole	kAsUEIA
15.	gasolinera	gas station	GAsOIInErA
16.	guerrilla	guerrilla	GERRIYA
17.	guisante	pea	GIsAntE
18.	pingüino	penguin	pInGUInO
19.	paragüero	umbrella stand	pArAGUErO
20.	golondrina	swallow	GOIOndrINΛ
21.	gusto	taste	GUstO
22.	general	general	HEnErAl
23.	girar	turn	HIirAr
24.	hotel	hotel	OtEl
25.	ratón	mouse	RRAtOn
26.	horror	horror	ORROr
27.	barro	mud	bARRO
28.	llama	flame	YAmA
29.	callado	quiet	kAYAdO
30.	cayado	walking stick	kAYAdO

Exercise 2.

The following table shows one example of each possible combination of vowel sound in Spanish. Using the symbols of exercise 1, write only the sound-value of each combination of vowels. For example, for "real," write EA.

	a	e	i	o	u
a	Aarón	aéroplano	baipás	cacao	audio
e	real	proveer	freír	león	Europa
i	familia	siete	chiita	violeta	ciudad
o	boa	bohemio	coincidencia	zoo	Ourense
u	cuatro	nueve	ruina	monstruo	duunviro

Translation of the table above.

	a	e	i	o	u
a	Aaron	airplane	bypass	cocoa	audio
e	real	to provide	to fry	lion	Europe
i	family	seven	Shia Muslim	violet	city
o	boa	bohemian	coincidence	zoo	Orense
u	four	nine	ruin	monster	duumviri

Answers:

	a	e	i	o	u
a	AA	AE	AI	AO	AU
e	EA	EE	EI	EO	EU
i	IA	IE	II	IO	IU
o	OA	OE	OI	OO	OU
u	UA	UE	UI	UO	UU

As you practiced in this exercised, Spanish assigns one symbol (a ,e ,i, o, u) to each vowel sound (A, E, I, O, U), so reading two vowels in sequence is just to read one symbol after the other.

2. ORTHOGRAPHY
ORTOGRAFÍA

Writing correctly implies knowing:

- the spelling of words: which letters form each word
- the accentuation: which word needs accent mark
- the capitalization: which word needs to be in upper case
- the punctuation: which other symbols the sentence needs, such as commas, etc.
- the composition: which organization in paragraphs makes the text more clear or expressive.

These five matters have very different level of difficulty, since the rules for capitalization, punctuation and composition don't vary much from the English counterparts. If you write effective compositions in English, you will write them well in Spanish.

This chapter focuses on spelling and accentuation, and it is divided into:

- Rules of Thumb on Spelling
- Spelling of the Grammatical Words
- Rules of Accents
- Composition, Capitalization, and Punctuation

Rules of Thumb on Spelling

Despite all efforts to make Spanish a phonetic-based language, there are some letters and combination of letters that are read the same (they have the same sound-value):

- b ↔ v
- ll ↔ y
- ge ↔ je, gi↔ ji
- s↔z
- ce↔se ↔ze, ci↔si↔zi
- que↔ ke, qui↔ ki
- ca↔ ka, co↔ ko, cu ↔ku
- h ↔ –

The Association of Academies of the Spanish Language (*La Asociación de Academias de la Lengua Española*) updates the Spanish dictionary, grammar and ortography. Its dictionary rules about the spelling on each word. Its criteria has to do with the sound of each word and, secondarily, with its original spelling. Thus, the word "hombre" (= man) has a "h" because the Latin word "*hominem*" has "h." However, with time, some rules have been established to help spell some sets of words.

Its book of Spanish Orthography (*Ortografía de la Lengua Española)* explains those rules, but neither those rules cover all cases (e.g. no rule explains why "hombre" has "h"), nor are all rules practical. For example, one rule says: "verbs ending with 'bir' sound have a 'b' with the exceptions of "hervir," "servir," "vivir" and their derivatives;" but among a set of 400 common verbs (listed in the book *Spanish for Californians*) there are only seven verbs ending in "bir" or "vir."

However, some basic rules can help you guess the right spelling in many cases. These are:

The "**rule zero**" or common rule on spelling is that every letter has a sound, and each word must sound as the sequence of letters that form it. Thus, if you pronounce the word /adicsión/ you should not write "**add**ición" because you don't pronounce the "d" twice; and if, for the first time, you see written "hotel" you should not pronounce the "h" as in English.

1. Pairs as "bb, dd, ff, pp, ss, tt, zz, sh, sr, ph" don't exist. Examples:

   efecto, abreviación, adicción* [not effecto, etc.]
   effect, abbreviation, addiction

(*) Notice that each "c" has a sound: /a-dik-sión/

2. Words can't start with letter "s" followed by a consonant. Examples:

    especial, España, estándar [not special, etc.]
    special, Spain, standard

3. K and W are very rarely used (karate, kimono, okey, waterpolo, Washington). Use C or Q for the k sound; and use: "gua, güe, güi, guo, gu" for the "w" sound. Examples:

    flanquear, noquear [not flankear, not nockear]
    to flank, to knock out

    guapo, güero, pingüino, antiguo [not wapo, not wero, etc.]
    handsome, blonde, penguin, old

4. Use "ce," "ci" instead of "ze," "zi." Examples:

    cero, cebra, empecé [not zero, not zebra, not empezé]
    zero, zebra, I started

5. The plural of words ending in "z" is "ces" (not "zes"). Examples:

    cruz, cruces, luz, luces, vez, veces [not cruzes, not luzes, etc.]
    cross, crosses, light, lights, time, times

6. Letter M (not N) comes before B or P. Examples:

    bomba, ambar, amplio, romper [not bonba, not anbar, etc.]
    bomb, amber, ample, to break

7. Words ending with "i" vowel sound in Spanish are spelled: ay, ey, oy, uy (not ai, ei, oi, ui), as long as the stress is not in the last vowel. Examples:

    ahí, rey*, reí, ley, leí, hoy, oí, ¡huy!, huí [not rei, lei, hoi, ¡hui!]
    there, king, I laughed, law, I read(past), today, I heard, ouch!, I fled

    (*) Underline indicates the point of stress

8. Words starting with vowel sounds "ua," "ue," "ui," "ia," and "ie" are spelled with "h:" hua, hue, hui, hia, hie. Examples:

    Huáscar, huevo, huir, hiato, hielo [not Uáscar, uevo, uir, iato, ielo]
    Huascar, egg, to flee, hiatus, ice

9. Words of the same family have similar spelling. Examples:

> hombre, humano, humanizar, humanidades [all with "h"]
> man, human, humanize, humanities

> hacer, haciendo, hecho, hice [all with "h"]
> to do, doing, done, I did

The exceptions are the words that start with "ua," "ue" "ui." Examples:

> orfanato, orfandad, huerfano [with "h" because it starts with ue]
> orphanage, orphanhood orphan

> ovalo, ovoide, ovario, huevo [with "h" because it starts with ue]
> oval, ovoid, ovary, egg

> oler, oliendo, oleré, huelo [with "h" because it starts with ue]
> to smell, smelling, I will smell, I smell

10. If the conjugation of a verb requires the Spanish ll/y or g/j, and its infinitive doesn't include the letters ll/y or g/j respectively, always use "y" and "j". Examples:

> cayendo, construyo [not callendo, not contrullendo]
> falling, I build

> dije, produje [not dige, not produge].
> I said, I produced

The *Diccionario de la Real Academia de la Lengua* establishes the correct spelling of all words. This dictionary is updated to include new words that a large number of speakers either adopt from other languages or create.

- Sometimes the new word is left as is or is adapted so that it will not conflict with the Spanish pronunciation. When this is the case, the word is written and treated as a Spanish word. For example:

> estándard, picnic, estrés, baipás, suéter, tabú
> standard, picnic, stress, bypass, sweater, taboo

- Other times the new word conflicts with the Spanish pronunciation. When this is the case, the word must be written in *italics* to indicate that it must have the foreign pronunciation. For example:

> *email, software, hardware, ballet, pizza, hobby*
> email, software, hardware, ballet, pizza, hobby

Spelling of the Grammatical Words

Certain words are repeatedly used in any speech, these are the words that make up the structure of the sentence. These words are the grammatical words:

- **Determiners** (determinantes): the, a, an, five, these, etc.
- **Pronouns** (pronombres): we, us, ours, ourselves, me, etc.
- **Prepositions** (preposiciones): of, for, at, on, in, under, etc.
- **Conjunctions** (conjunciones): and, or, yet, but, what, if, etc.
- **Auxiliary Verbs** (verbos auxiliares): am, be, have, has, etc.

The non grammatical words are the rest of the types:

- **Non-auxiliary Verbs** (verbos no auxiliares): worked, proven, etc.
- **Adjectives** (adjetivos): green, large, true, productive, etc.
- **Nouns** (nombres): Peter, house, truth, productivity, etc.
- **Adverbs** (adverbios) rapidly, quietly, strongly, etc.
- **Interjections** (interjecciones): hello, bye, etc.

It is highly recommended that you test your spelling on these words through a dictation. For this goal, this book includes *Appendix D: List of Grammatical Words*. This list includes some interjections because of their very frequent use.

Notice that some words can have the same pronunciation (identical or different because of the accent) and different spelling in order to show different meaning. For example:

Spanish	English	Example
a	to	Él va a Perú hoy (= He goes to Peru today.)
ha	has	Él ha ido a Perú. (= He has gone to Peru.)
hay	there is/are	Hay un problema. (= There is a problem.)
¡Ay!	Ouch!	¡Ay! Eso duele. (= Ouch! That hurts.)
ahí	there	Puedo verlo ahí. (= I can see it there.)
porqué	the reason	No conozco el porqué (= I don't know the reason.)
porque	because	No voy porque no quiero. (= I don't go because I don't want to.)
por qué	Why?	¿Por qué no vas? (= Why don't you go?)
por que	so that	Me fui por que no se pusiera nervioso. (= I left so that he didn't get nervous.)

Spanish	English	Example
sino	but (negat.)	No es un regalo sino un préstamo. (= It is not a present but a loan.)
si no	If not	Si no vienes, me enojaré. (= If you don't come, I will get angry.)

In the next section, Rules of Accents, you will find more words that have accent marks or not depending on their meaning, e.g. él/ el (= he/ the).

Spelling of the verbs

Similar to the grammatical words, the endings of the verbs are repeatedly used in a common speech. This is why it is highly recommended that you test yourself through a dictation. For this goal, this book includes *Appendix E Table of Endings of Regular Verbs.*

Rules of Accents

So far, you know how to pronounce the sound of a word but maynot know the right intonation of it. It's not the same to say "dessert" and "desert," or import and "import." Every word has a point of emphasis or stress.

The rules of the **accent marks** are especially useful for foreigners. With them you will be able to read any word on your own, without having listened to it before. In turn, you will be able to learn your own words from the dictionary without help.

Golden Rule

> All words, with no exception, have one, and only one, point of **stress**, and this always falls on a vowel (never on a consonant).
> The **accent marks** (á, é, í, ó, ú) indicate where the stressed vowel is.
> However, the majority of words don't require an **accent mark**.

In the following examples, you will see the underline to indicate where the stress of a word is when the accent mark is not used.

The rules of accent marks are simple to learn, once you know how to break down a word into syllables.

Breakdown of Words into Syllables

Unlike English, in Spanish the breakdown of words into syllables is very intuitive.

> ca-rro, ga-to, cla-se, ac-tor, a-pén-di-ce
> (= car, cat, class, actor, appendix)

What will need some explanation are the words with syllables that have two or more vowels. For instance, you need to know why "vio" (= I saw) has one syllable and "león" (= lion) has two (le-ón).

There are four elemental rules for syllabication:

- Every syllable has **at least** one vowel: a, e, i, o, u.

- Only the following pair of consonants must be together in the same syllable:

bl	cl	---	fl	gl	pl	tl
br	cr	dr	fr	gr	pr	tr

  And the single-sound pairs: **ch**, **ll**, **rr**.

  E.g. "**blanco**" (= white) can only be split into blan-co, since "bl" cannot be separate ("bl" is one of the pairs of the above), and since "nc" cannot be together (it is not any of the pairs of the above table).

- Two vowels will stay in the same syllable if at least one of them is a weak vowel. Classification of vowels:

  > a, e, o: strong vowels
  > i, u: weak vowels (the "sticky ones")

  Weak vowels create diphthongs, which is two vowels in the same syllable.

  Rule of thumb: weak vowels tend to be "sticky" and sticks to the vowels next to them in the same syllable.

Below, you will see this in all possible combination of vowels:

	a	e	i/ -y	o	u
a	A-a-rón	ca-er	h**ay**	va-ho	**áu**-re-o
e	re-al	le-er	l**ey**	le-ón	**Eu**-ro-pa
i/ -y	re-c**io**	s**ie**-te	chi-i-ta	mer-cu-r**io**	c**iu**-dad
o	ca-no-a	ro-er	h**oy**	di-cién-do-os	Ou-ren-se
u	c**ua**-tro	n**ue**-ve	r**ui**-na	an-ti-g**uo**	du-un-vi-ro

The rule of thumb above is also applicable to those few words that
have three vowels in a row. e.g. U-ru-g**uay**. The translation of those
words (if you are curious) is below:

	a	e	i/ -y	o	u
a	Aaron	to fall	there is	steam	golden
e	real	to read	law	lion	Europe
i/ -y	strong	seven	Shia Muslim	mercury	city
o	canoe	to gnaw	today	telling you guys (Spain)	Orense
u	four	nine	ruin	old	duumvir

- However, if the pair has a weak and a strong vowel and the word has the
  stress on the weak one, then the pair gets separated into two syllables. E.g.
  día → dí-a (= day)

Rules of Accents

Remember: all words in Spanish have one, and only one, point of stress, and
this always falls on a vowel. The accent mark is a mark of the stress.

The syllable that carries the stressed vowel is called the stressed syllable.

The first three rules that follow are called General Rules. These rules should
be learned first; the others are their amendments.

General Rules

One. If the stress is on the **last syllable**, and the word ends with a VOWEL, or N or S; then the word will have an accent mark.

> autobús, Ceilán, Perú, adiós, televisión
> bus, Ceylon, Peru, bye, television

> Examples of words with **no** accent mark: actor, actriz, cancelar, reloj
> (= actor, actress, to cancel, clock)

Two. If the stress is on the **second to last** and the word does **not** end with a VOWEL, N, or S, then it will have an accent mark.

> álbum, suéter, móvil, mármol, Pérez.
> album, sweater, mobile, marble, Perez.

> Examples of words with **no** accent mark: carro, torre, perfecto
> (= car, tower, perfect).

Three. If the stress is on the **third to last syllable or earlier**, it will have an accent mark, regardless of other considerations.

> apéndice, lógico, rígido, lámpara, búlgaro, teléfono, electrónico.
> appendix, logical, rigid, lamp, Bulgarian, telephone, electronic

> **Notice** that the counting of syllables starts from the end to the beginning: last, second to last, third to last (not first, second, third).

Complementary Rules

Four. When the two conditions below exist, it will have an accent mark.
> 1. the stress is on a syllable with a strong vowel followed by a weak vowel (ai, ei, oi, au, eu, ou), or vice versa (ia, ie, io, ua, ue, uo, iu, ui), or two different weak vowels (ui, iu)
> **and**
> 2. the vowel with the stress is a weak vowel

> Examples:

> día, caído, búho, río, ríe, día, baúl, Seúl, biografía, García, oído.

> day, fallen, owl, I laugh, he laughs, day, trunk, Seoul, biography,
>   Garcia, hear

This rule supercedes the previous ones.

Five. Single-syllable words will **not** have an accent mark.

E.g. voz, mar, sol, y, o, buey (= voice, ocean, sun, and, or, ox)

The exceptions of these rules are showed next.

Six. There is a list of words that have accents in order to distinguish two meanings. For example: "sí" (= yes) and "si" (= if) sound identical. The accent mark is used to leave clear which is which.

This rule supersedes the previous ones. These words are:

Spanish	English
el / él	the / he
tu / tú	your / you
mi / mí	my / me (as in "for me")
que / qué	"what" in sentences that are not questions or exclamations, as in "This is what I want."/ "what" in sentences that are questions or exclamations, as in "What is that?"
cual / cuál	which / which (same differentiation as with "what")
quien / quién	who / who (same differentiation as with "what")
donde / dónde	where / where (same differentiation as with "what")
cuando / cuándo	when / when (same differentiation as with "what")
como / cómo	as / how
si / sí	if / yes
aun / aún	even / still
mas / más	but / more
de / dé	of / "I give" (subjunctive)
se / sé	himself, herself, themselves / I know
te / té	your/ tea

Seven. Other considerations." In words ending in "mente" (suffix "-ly") you have to remove the suffix in order to apply the rules above. E.g. fácilmente, calmadamente. (= easily, calmly)

The Rules of Accents were created with the goal of having the lowest number of words requiring accent marks. For example, one-syllable words don't have an accent mark (Rule Five).

Either explicitly or implicitly, the rules of accents tell you where the stress is. For example, "transporte" (= transportation)

"Transporte" could be: | transporte
                          | transporte
                          | transporte

- If it were transporte, it would have an accent mark (Rule Three)
- If it were transporte, it would have an accent mark (Rule One)

Consequently, since "transporte" does not have an accent mark, the pronunciation will be: transporte.

Composition, Capitalization, and Punctuation

Composition

The following are just three practical rules on breaking down in paragraphs, indentation, and lists.

The paragraph ("párrafo" in Spanish) is the unit of speech. Every paragraph must correspond to one idea.

Indentation ("tabulación" in Spanish) is necessary in the first line of a paragraph. The exception is when you leave a blank line between paragraphs. With no indentation or blank line, you couldn't distinguish one paragraph from the other when the first paragraph happens to finish at the end of the line.

As English, lists of ideas in bullets ("topos" in Spanish) must have a parallel structure. For example:

> There are three main internet browsers:
> - Windows Explorer [a noun]
> - Apple Safari [a noun]
> - Google Chrome [a noun]

No:

> There are three main internet browsers:
> - Windows Explorer, the most widely used [noun and comment]
> - Apple Safari is the only compatible with Macintosh [sentence]
> - Google Chrome [a noun]

Capitalization

You must capitalize in the following cases:

- at the beginning of a text
- after a stop or full stop
- in names of people and places, e.g. Juan, Perú
- in titles of works, as books, documents, etc., e.g. *Don Quijote.*
- **not** for adjectives of cultures, peoples, languages, etc. (unlike English) e.g. español (not Español)

With titles, it is common to capitalize just the main words: the initial word and nouns, adjectives, adverbs and verbs.

In addition, names of major literary works (novels, books of poems, or books of essays) are in italics. Minor works, such as short stories, poems, or brief essays, are in quotation marks.

> El libro *Cien Años de Soledad* es un clásico.
> The book *One Hundred Years of Solitude* is a classic.

Punctuation

The punctuation symbols are:

English	Spanish	Symbol
period	punto	.
comma	coma	,
colon	dos puntos	:
semicolon	punto y coma	;
ellipsis	puntos suspensivos	...
parenthesis	paréntesis	( )
square brackets	corchetes	[ ]
dash (short dash)	guión	-
dash (long dash)	raya	—
quotation marks	comillas	" " ` ´ « »
question mark	signos de interrogación	¿ ?
exclamation mark	signos de exclamación	¡ !

Other punctuation marks, as brackets [ ] {}, apostrophe ' , section sign §, asterisk *, and slash / , have the same use both in Spanish and English.

Unlike English, in Spanish, if there are two punctuation symbols together, then periods, commas, semicolons, colons go after parenthesis, squared brackets, dash or quotation marks.

> Dijo: "Hola".
> He said: "Hi."

1.   Period

Uses	Examples
▪ At the end of a sentence.	Ayer llovió. (= Yesterday it rained.)
▪ In abbreviations	e.g. (= exempla gratia), univ. (= university), EE.UU. * (= United States)
▪ **not** used in titles even if the title is a whole sentence	El libro *La Sombra del Ciprés es Alargada* fue el primer éxito de Miguel Delibes. = The book *The Shadow of the Cypress is Elongated* was the first success of Miguel Delibes.

(*) In Spanish two-word plural acronyms are formed by repeating the initials separated by periods, i.e. Juegos Olimpicos → JJ.OO. (= Olympic Games)

2.   Comma

Uses	Examples
▪ to set off the vocative	Pedro, ven aquí. (= Pedro, come here)
▪ within a list, to separate its elements with the exception of the last conjunction as "y, o, ni" (= and, or, nor). However, a comma is used in front of a conjunction when the conjunction introduces <u>a clause that is not part of the list.</u>	Pedro, Antonio, Juan y Luis vinieron. (=Pedro, Antonio, Juan, and Luis came). Pintaron las paredes, movieron los muebles, <u>y quedaron encantados</u>. (= They paint the walls, moved the furniture, and they loved it).
▪ to set off <u>nonrestrictive clauses</u>	María, <u>la hermana de Claudia</u>, no vino. (=Maria, Claudia's sister, didn't come).
▪ when the natural order of the sentence is altered. However a comma is not used when <u>the object</u> is followed by the verb.	Honor, ya no tiene. [instead of: Ya no tiene honor.] (= He no longer has honor]. <u>A las tres hermanas</u> vi. [instead of: Vi a las tres hermanas. (= I saw the three sisters)
▪ before conjunctions such as "pero, así que, pues" (= but, so, for)	Me gusta el abrigo, pero me queda pequeño. (= I like the coat, but it's small). Esto no me gusta, así que me voy. (= I don't like this, so I go).
▪ After links such as "finalmente, efectivamente, no obstante," "es decir" (= at last, that's it, nevertheless, this means)	Efectivamente, es necesario. (= that's it, it's necessary) Son sinónimos, es decir, significan lo mismo. (= They are synonims, that is, they mean the same).
▪ to substitute a verb that is omitted.	Juan perdió su sinceridad; su esposa, el amor. [instead of: Juan perdió su sinceridad; su esposa perdió el amor] (= Juan lost his sincerity; his wife lost her love.)
▪ **Never** setting off the <u>subject</u> from <u>verb</u>.	<u>Pedro fue</u> a la fiesta.

3.   Colon

Uses	Examples
▪ to set off a list of elements	Los puntos cardinales son: norte, sur, este y oeste. OR: Norte, sur, este y oeste: estos son los puntos cardinales. (= The cardinal points are north, south, east and west).
▪ Before a quote	Pedro dijo: "Sí quiero". (= Peter said: "I do.")
▪ Before an example	Deben escribir algo sobre un animal curioso: la zarigüeya. (= You must write something about a strange animal: the opossum)
▪ To connect sentences and avoid using conjunctions	No tengo dinero: no podré ir de vacaciones. (= I don't have money, so I won't be able to go on vacations)

4.   Semicolon

Uses	Examples
▪ To set off elements within a complex list that already has commas.	El abrigo era azul; los pantalones, blancos; y los zapatos, negros. (= The coat was blue, the pants were white, and the shoes were black).
▪ Before conjunctions such as "pero, sin embargo" (= but, however), when the clauses are long.	Su discurso estuvo muy bien construido; sin embargo no consiguió convencer a su audiencia. (= His speech was very well built; however he was not able to convince his audience)

5. Dash

Spanish distinguishes between long and short dash (raya and guion). The long dash is used as a parenthesis, and also in dialogues (English uses quotation marks instead).

> — Sí. [without closing dashes]
> — Sí — contestó Pedro.
> — Sí — contestó Juan — pero con mis condiciones.

> "Yes."
> "Yes" - answered Pedro
> "Yes" - answered Juan-, "but with my conditions".

The short dash is used to divide compound words, as lógico-crítico (= logical-critical).

6. Quotation marks

They can be: "x", «x» or `x.´ Different types must be used when one quoted fragment is within a larger quoted fragment.

Other symbols (periods, comma, etc.) always go after the quotation marks (unlike English).

7. Question marks

Questions must be "opened" (¿) and "closed" (?). The beginning of questions must be placed where the intonation of the question actually starts, not necessarily at the beginning of the sentence.

> Por favor ¿puedes hacerlo por mí?
> Please, can you do it for me?

8. Exclamation marks

Exclamation must be "opened" (¡) and "closed" (!). The beginning of exclamation must be placed where the intonation of the exclamation actually starts, and not necessarily at the beginning of the sentence.

> Dijo "¡estupendo!" y lo hizo.
> He said, "Great!" and did it.

Frequently Asked Questions

FAQ 1: Again, what is the difference between accent mark and stress?

Stress is the elevation of intonation of a vowel in the word. An accent mark is the mark that indicates that stress. In Spanish, every word has one, and only one, stressed vowel; however, most of the words don't have an accent mark. The term "accent" is confusing since it may mean either "stress" or "accent mark." Normally "accent" refers to "accent mark."

This book uses the underline to mark the stress in those words that have no accent mark.

FAQ 2: Vídeo or Video?

Just a few words can be pronounced with different stress. This is the case of vídeo/ video (= video, video tape, DVR) or período/periodo (= period). You must choose one or the other to be consistent with your dialect.

FAQ 3: Do I really need to learn how to break the words into syllables?

Only if you want to learn the rules of accents. These rules are based on syllables.

FAQ 4: How do I know where the stress is in words like "construimos," which has two vowels together in the stressed syllable?

In Spanish, when two weak vowels (i and u) are found together in the stressed syllable, the stress is always on the second vowel: cons-tru-i-mos (= we build/ we built). Another example: hu-ir (= to flee)

Exercises

Exercise 1

The following list includes 60 misspelled Spanish words. Rewrite them correctly and write the number of the rule by which it has that spelling (the numbering is that of the section Rules of Thumb on Spelling). If the misspelled word doesn't sound right according to the norms of pronunciation (rule zero), write "0."

If the misspelled word is a grammatical word (including auxiliary verbs and verb endings) write g.w.

#	Spanish error	English	Answer	Rule
1	abbreviación	abbreviation	abreviación	g.w.
2	haver	to have	haber	g.w.
3	addicción	addiction	adicción	1
4	ahý	there	ahí	7
5	alrrededor	around	alrededor	0
6	aparcarr	to park	aparcar	0
7	attribuir	to attribute	atribuir	1
8	Bombai	Bombay	Bombay	7
9	bonba	pump	bomba	6
10	boy	I go	voy	g.w.
11	buei	ox	buey	7
12	callendo	falling	cayendo	10
13	camviar	to change	cambiar	6
14	canpo	field	campo	6
15	cantávamos	we sang	cantábamos	g.w.
16	cantaz	you sing	cantas	g.w.
17	cantaze	…(that) I sang	cantase	g.w.
18	carrta	letter	carta	0
19	conpañero	companion	compañero	6
20	consequencias	consequences	consecuencias	0
21	cruzes	crosses	cruces	5
22	effecto	effect	efecto	1
23	estoi	I am	estoy	g.w.
24	fueze	…(that) I was	fuese	g.w.
25	güisante	pea	guisante	0
26	hoý	I heard	oí	7

#	Spanish error	English	Answer	Rule
27	huý	I fled	huí	7
28	iato	hiatus	hiato	8
29	iena	hyena	hiena	8
30	iere	it hurts	hiere	8
31	Irack	Iraq	Irak	0
32	kómodo	comfortable	cómodo	3
33	lei	law	ley	7
34	lelló	he read (past)	leyó	10
35	leý	I read (past)	leí	7
36	llendo	going	yendo	10
37	luzes	lights	luces	5
38	massa	mass	masa	1
39	nino	child	niño	0
40	oyremos	hear	oiremos	9
41	paraguero	umbrella stand	paragüero	0
42	pinguino	penguin	pingüino	0
43	questionario	questionnaire	cuestionario	0
44	rei	king	rey	7
45	reý	I laughed	reí	7
46	rratón	mouse	ratón	0
47	rrebelión	rebellion	rebelión	0
48	sfera	sphere	esfera	2
49	soi	am	soy	g.w.
50	spléndido	splendid	espléndido	2
51	stratosfera	stratosphere	estratosfera	2
52	uele	smells	huele	8
53	uir	escape	huir	8
54	Uruguai	Uruguay	Uruguay	7
55	vozes	voices	voces	5
56	zeamos	Let's be	seamos	g.w.
57	zebra	zebra	cebra	4
58	zelos	jealousy	celos	4
59	zerilla	match	cerilla	4
60	zero	zero	cero	4

Exercise 2

In the first table below, divide the words into syllables (translation is provided in the second table).

	a	e	i	o	u
a	Aarón	aéreo	ahí	ahora	aún
e	marea	creer	rey	neón	eureka
i	diario	viejo	chiita	violeta	viuda
o	boa	roedor	soy	zoo	Ourense
u	cuadro	hueso	huir	búho	duunviro

	a	e	i	o	u
a	Aaron	airborne	there	now	still
e	tide	to believe	king	neon	eureka
i	daily	old	Shia Muslim	violet	widow
o	boa	rodent	I am	zoo	Orense
u	painting	bone	to flee	owl	duumviri

Answers:

	a	e	i	o	u
a	A-a-rón	a-é-re-o	a-hí*	a-ho-ra	a-ún*
e	ma-re-a	cre-er	rey	ne-ón	eu-re-ka
i	dia-rio	vie-jo	chi-i-ta	vio-le-ta	viu-da
o	bo-a	ro-e-dor	soy	zo-o	Ou-ren-se
u	cua-dro	hue-so	huir	bú-ho*	du-un-vi-ro

(*) The stress is on the weak vowel of the pair, that is why the syllable split (fourth Rule of Accents).

Notice that you can test yourself on accent marks by looking at the words of the vocabulary at the end of each chapter, since all those words have the stressed vowel underlined.

Exercise 3

Put the accent mark where appropriate in the following sayings and sentences:

1. Quien rie el ultimo, rie mejor. (Literally: Who laughs last, laughs best)

2. Cada cual cuenta la feria como le fue. (Literally: Each person tells about the fair as he did).

3. Casa de dos puertas, dificil de guardar. (Literally: A house with two doors is difficult to protect)

4. Cria cuervos y te sacaran los ojos. (Literally: Raise crows and they will take your eyes out)

5. Mas vale pajaro en mano que ciento volando. (Literally: Better a bird in hand than one hundred flying)

6. Quien a buen arbol se arrima, buena sombra le cobija. (Literally: Who comes closer to a good tree, its shade protects him).

7. El no puede venir. (= He can't come)

8. Tu perro ladra demasiado. (= Your dog barks too much)

9. Te es mi bebida favorita. (= Tea is my favorite drink).

10. "Si, quiero" -dijo Pedro sin dudar. (= "Yes, I do," said Pedro without hesitation)

11. Se que es un error. (= I know it is an error).

12. Que no. (= Again, no)

13. ¡Quien lo diria! (= Who said)

14. ¿Cual prefieres? (= Which one do you prefer?)

15. ¿Donde quieres que lo deje? (= Where do you want me to leave it?)

16. Como lo vi, te lo cuento (= As I saw it, I tell you)

Answers

1. Quien ríe el ultimo, ríe mejor.

2. Cada cual cuenta la feria como le fue.

3. Casa de dos puertas, difícil de guardar.

4. Cría cuervos y te sacarán los ojos.

5. Más vale pájaro en mano que ciento volando.

6. Quien a buen árbol se arrima, buena sombra le cobija.

7. Él no puede venir.

8. Tu perro ladra demasiado.

9. Té es mi bebida favorita.

10. "Sí, quiero" -dijo Pedro sin dudar.

11. Sé que es un error.

12. Que no.

13. ¡Quién lo diría!

14. ¿Cuál prefieres?

15. ¿Dónde quieres que lo deje?

16. Como lo vi, te lo cuento

Exercise 4

Put the accent mark where appropriate in the following words of the column
Spanish and write the rule by which the accent mark has to be placed or not.
(Note: underline indicates stress)

#	Spanish	English	Answer	Rule
1	autobus	bus	autobús	1
2	actor	actor	actor	1
3	arbol	tree	árbol	2
4	mesa	table	mesa	2
5	apendice	appendix	apéndice	3
6	con	with	con	5
7	dia	day	día	4
8	diario	diary, daily	diario	2
9	santuario	sanctuary	santuario	2
10	estan	they are	están	1
11	actriz	actress	actriz	1
12	album	album	álbum	2
13	torre	tower	torre	2
14	lampara	lamp	lámpara	2
15	voy	I go	voy	5
16	buho	owl	búho	4
17	oido	ear	oído	4
18	airear	to air out	airear	1
19	Peru	Peru	Perú	1
20	reloj	clock	reloj	1
21	cesped	grass	césped	2

#	Spanish	English	Response	Rule
22	perfecto	perfect	perfecto	2
23	teléfono	phone	teléfono	3
24	ser	to be	ser	5

Exercise 5

Put the accent mark where appropriate in the following verb forms of the column **Spanish** (underline indicates stress):

#	Spanish	English	Answer	Rule
1	cante	…that I sing	cante	2
2	cante	I sang	canté	1
3	cantabamos	we were singing	cantábamos	3
4	cantare	I will sing	cantaré	1
5	canto	S/he sang	cantó	1
6	estaba	I was	estaba	2
7	seamos	…that we be	seamos	2
8	cantaria	I would sing	cantaría	4
9	cantais	you guys (Spain)	cantáis	1
10	canto	I sing	canto	2
11	cantaras	…that you sing	cantaras	2
12	voy	I go	voy	5
13	fui	I went, I was	fui	5
14	cantaramos	…that we sang	cantáramos	3
15	cantado	sung	cantado	2
16	¡Canta!	Sing!	¡Canta!	2
17	cantando	singing	cantando	2
18	cantar	to sing	cantar	1
19	habia	he had…	había	4
20	eramos	we were	éramos	3

Exercise 6

Put the appropriate punctuation and capital letters in the following sentences:

1. pedro juan y luis fueron a la fiesta
2. es cierto que lucas mi amigo es mexicano de veracruz
3. la chaqueta es azul los pantalones blancos y el abrigo negro
4. juanito ven aquí
5. él dijo el libro titulado niebla es mi favorito
6. por favor puedes hacerlo   [question]
7. me gusta ese abrigo pero es demasiado pequeño
8. los puntos cardinales son norte sur este y oeste

Answers:

1. Pedro, Juan y Luis fueron a la fiesta.

   Pedro, Juan, y Luis went to the party.

2. Es cierto que Lucas, mi amigo, es mexicano de Veracruz.

   It is true that Lucas, my friend, is Mexican from Veracruz.

3. La chaqueta es azul; los pantalones, blancos; y el abrigo, negro.

   The jacket is blue; the pants, white; and the coat, black.

4. Juanito, ven aquí.

   Juanito, come here.

5. "El dijo" el libro titulado *Niebla* es mi favorito".

   He said: "the book *Niebla* is my favorite."

6. Por favor ¿puedes hacerlo?

   Please, can you do it?

7. Me gusta ese abrigo, pero es demasiado pequeño.

   I like that coat but it's too small.

8. Los puntos cardinales son: norte, sur, este y oeste.

   The four cardinal directions are: north, south, east, and west.

3. ADJECTIVES
ADJETIVOS

According to their functions in the sentence, words can be:

- **Interjections** (interjecciones): Hello, Bye...
- **Determiners** (determinantes): the, a, an, five, these...
- **Adjectives** (adjetivos): green, large, true, productive...
- **Nouns** (nombres): Peter, house, truth, productivity...
- **Pronouns** (pronombres): we, us, ours, ourselves, me...
- **Adverbs** (adverbios) rapidly, quietly, strongly...
- **Prepositions** (preposiciones): of, for, at, on, in, under...
- **Conjunctions** (conjunciones): and, or, yet, but, what, if...
- **Verbs** (verbos): am, have, goes, worked, forgotten...

Let's see one example in one sentence:

Wow! that gray dog that she bought in Germany runs fast!
INTERJ. DET. ADJ. NOUN CONJ PRON. VERB PREP. NOUN VERB ADVERB

You just need to know that each type of word identifies a function, and that a word can have different roles in different sentences. In the following example, the word "milk" has different uses.

Noun: **Milk** is the product from cows.
Adjective   **Milk** products sell well.
Verb: The farmers **milk** the cows everyday.

The above classification of words overlaps that of grammatical words and non-grammatical words. **Grammatical words** are: determiners, pronouns, prepositions, conjunctions, a few adverbs, and the auxiliary verbs (as to have,

to be and to go). **Non-grammatical words** are: interjections, nouns,
adjectives, most adverbs, and verbs.

Some books on English grammar consider **determiners** as a type of **adjective**
based on their similarities. However, when learning Spanish, distinguishing
the difference is important. In Spanish, the determiner goes before the noun,
and the adjective after the noun. In English, both the determiner and adjective
go before the noun.

> Many violet flowers
> DET.   ADJ.

> Muchas flores violetas
> DET.   ADJ.

You may be familiar with the term "article" as a type of word. Articles are the
words "the," a," "an," and they are a type of "determiners."

You may also be familiar with the term "possessive." This is a subtype of
words as well. This label is ambiguous since there are: possessive determiners
(as "my"), possessive pronouns (as "mine"), etc.

The following table displays the most important features of each type of
words. You will learn more in detail in next chapters.

Type	Gramm. Words?	Masc./ fem.	Singu./ plural	Person & tense
Interjections	no	no	no	no
Determiners	yes	yes	yes	no
Adjectives	no	yes	yes	no
Nouns	no	yes (**)	yes	no
Pronouns	yes	yes	yes	no
Adverbs	a few (*)	no	no	no
Prepositions	yes	no	no	no
Conjunctions	yes	no	no	no
Verbs	a few (*)	no	no	yes

(*) Because of their grammatical value we can consider grammatical
words adverbs like "muy" (= very), "aquí" (= here), and the four
auxiliary verbs: "ser," "estar" (both meaning "to be"), haber (= to
have) and "ir" (= to go).

(**) Nouns have an intrinsic gender. They have a fixed gender: either
masculine or feminine. Other types, as the determiners, have both.

Definitions

Adjectives are the words that inform us about qualities of the noun or pronoun, e.g. blue, large, expensive, happy, etc.

Unlike Spanish, **in English**, adjectives are classified into two main kinds:

- **Descriptive adjectives**, which give concrete information about the noun, as: blue, large, expensive, or happy. As a rule of thumb: descriptive adjectives are the adjectives that can go after the verb "to be," e.g. "His house will be blue.

- **Limiting adjectives**, which give more grammatical information rather than descriptive, as: more, all, two, or some.

Spanish grammar only consider "adjectives" the first type above (descriptive adjectives); the second type are not considered adjectives, but determiners. In Spanish, determiners go always before the nouns (e.g. "más personas"); unlike adjectives (e.g. "personas importantes").

In addition, in Spanish and English, the past participle (e.g. written, forgotten, tired) is a form of the verb (to write, to forget, to tire) that can function as an adjective. When so, it follows the same rules as the adjectives. For example: in the same way that a test can be "easy," and the word "easy" is an adjective, a test can be "written"(instead of oral) and the word "written" functions as an adjective.

Some written tests
Unos exámenes escritos

The table of "escrito" is:

	SINGULAR	PLURAL
MASCULINE	**escrito**	escritos
FEMININE	escrita	escritas

This chapter will only analyze the **descriptive adjectives**, in other words, the Spanish adjectives, and this is the name that will be used throughout the text.

The two relevant features of the Spanish adjectives are: 1) gender and number, and 2) placement.

Gender and Number of Spanish Adjectives

Adjectives follow the noun in number (singular/plural) and in gender (masculine/ feminine).

The way adjectives form the feminine depends on the masculine form, according to these rules:

- The adjectives that end in "-o" (in the masculine-singular form) form the feminine by switching the "-o" to an "-a."

	SINGULAR	PLURAL
MASCULINE	-o	-os
FEMININE	-a	-as

For example "rojo"(= red):

	SINGULAR	PLURAL
MASCULINE	rojo	rojos
FEMININE	roja	rojas

- The adjectives that don't end with "-o" (in the masculine-singular form) will have the same form for masculine and feminine. For example "verde" (= green):

	SINGULAR	PLURAL
MASCULINE	verde	verdes
FEMININE	verde	verdes

Other examples are: "violeta" and "importante" (= violet, important):

	SINGULAR	PLURAL
MASCULINE	violeta	violetas
FEMININE	violeta	violetas

	SINGULAR	PLURAL
MASCULINE	importante	importantes
FEMININE	importante	importantes

The main exception to this rule are the adjectives related to nationalities, for which you have to add an "a" to make the feminine form.

inglés	ingleses	= English
inglesa	inglesas	
japonés	japoneses	= Japanese
japonesa	japonesas	
alemán	alemanes	= German
alemana	alemanas	
español	españoles	= Spanish
española	españolas	
portugués	portugueses	= Portuguese
portuguesa	portuguesas	
danés	daneses	= Danish
danesa	danesas	
francés	franceses	= French
francesa	francesas	
irlandés	irlandeses	= Irish
irlandesa	irlandesas	
ceilanés	ceilaneses	= Sri Lankan
ceilanesa	ceilanesas	
neocelandés	neocelandeses	= New Zealander
neocelandesa	neocelandesas	
finlandés	finlandeses	= Finish
finlandesa	finlandesas	

(*) Remember that, in Spanish, the adjectives of places (inglés, japonés, etc.) are not capitalized.

Regarding the concordance of number (singular/plural), the basic rule is:

- If the adjective ends with a vowel (a, e, i, o, u) you will have to add "s." Example:

	SINGULAR	PLURAL
MASCULINE	**rojo**	rojos
FEMININE	roja	rojas

- Otherwise you will add "es." If the adjective ends with "z," you will change the "z" into a c." For example "azul" and "audaz" (= blue, audacious):

	SINGULAR	PLURAL
MASCULINE	**azul**	azules
FEMININE	azul	azules

	SINGULAR	PLURAL
MASCULINE	**audaz**	audaces
FEMININE	audaz	audaces

Notice that "audaz" doesn't change in the feminine since it doesn't end with "o."

Finally there are adjectives that change neither gender nor number. This is the case of:

- the adjectives: "macho"(= male) and "hembra" (= female)

	SINGULAR	PLURAL
MASCULINE	**macho**	macho
FEMININE	macho	macho

Tenemos un sapo macho, dos sapos macho y dos ranas hembra.
We have one male toad, two male toads, and two female frogs.

- The adjectives that follow the words: "tipo" (= type), "color" (= color), or "modelo" (= model).

El complejo consta de cuatro cas**as** tipo español [no "españolas"]
The condominium consists of four Spanish-type houses

He comprado dos furgonet**as** color amarillo, modelo italiano
I have bought two yellow-color italian-model vans.

- The first word of compound adjectives. In this case the word is hyphenated and the first adjective is always masculine and singular.

Tuvieron lugar varias reacciones físico-químicas.
Some physicochemical reactions occurred.

Placement of Spanish Adjectives

In general, Spanish adjectives go after the noun. For example:

La casa roja
The red house

However, there are four exceptions where the adjective can be placed after the noun.

1. The adjectives *bueno, malo, primero, tercero,* and *grande*

These five adjectives are commonly placed before the noun.

Esa es la **tercera** casa [more common].
Esa es la casa **tercera** [less common].
That is the third house.

When they are placed before the noun, **and the noun is masculine-singular**, then they lose the last letters (This is called "*apócope*"= shortening).

Ese es el **tercer** piso [more common].
Ese es el piso **tercero** [less common].
That is the third floor.

The list of adjectives that can be shortened are:

	SINGULAR	PLURAL	
MASCULINE	bueno, buen	buenos	= good
FEMININE	buena	buenas	
MASCULINE	malo, mal	malos	= bad
FEMININE	mala	malas	
MASCULINE	primero, primer	primeros	= first
FEMININE	primera	primeras	
MASCULINE	tercero, tercer	terceros	⁻ third
FEMININE	tercera	terceras	
MASCULINE	grande, gran	grandes	= big great*
FEMININE	grande, **gran**	grandes	

As you can see in the table, they are only shortened in the masculine-singular form, **with the exception of "grande,"** which is shortened to "gran" in the masculine-singular and feminine-singular form.

Notice that these adjectives follow the rule of construction of feminine studied above: bueno, malo, primero, and tercero end with an "o", so their feminine will end with an "a", and the plural forms will end with "os" and "as." And "grande," doesn't end with an "o", so its feminine form is the same as its masculine form.

2. The adjectives that change their meaning

There is a list of Spanish adjectives that change their meaning if they are placed after the noun.

Spanish	English	Nuance when preceding	Nuance when following
antiguo	old	former	old-fashioned
bajo	short	vile	short in size, vile
medio	half, average	half	average
nuevo	new	different	brand new
pobre	poor	unfortunate	without money
puro	pure	total	purified
único	only, unique	only	unique
viejo	old	aged	not young

Examples:

Mi antiguo carro era rojo.
My former car was red.

Me gustan los carros antiguos.
I like old-fashioned cars.

La envidia es un bajo sentimiento (bajo).
Envy is a low feeling.

Pedro es un hombre bajo.
Pedro is a short person.

Juan es un viejo amigo. Le conozco desde el primer grado.
Juan is an old friend. I know him from first grade.

Arturo es un ingeniero viejo. Tiene 60 años.
Arturo is an old engineer. He is 60-year old

3. The adjectives that can either describe or limit the noun.

In ambiguous sentences where the adjective can either describe the noun or limit the noun, Spanish places the adjective:

- before the noun, when describing the noun
- after the noun, when limiting the noun

Example:

> Los distinguidos soldados de Julio Cesar desfilaron en
> Roma.
> (All) The distinguished soldiers of Julius Caesar marched
> in Rome.

> Los soldados distinguidos de Julio Cesar desfilaron en
> Roma.
> (Only) The distinguished soldiers of Julius Caesar marched
> in Rome.

Frequently Asked Questions

FAQ 1: Why is the classification of words important?

Every type of words represents one function in the sentence, and has different properties. Thanks to that categorization, we can make statements like:

- Nouns have an intrinsic gender.
- Adjectives and determiners correspond to the noun in number (singular, plural) and gender (masculine, feminine).
- Adjectives go after the nouns.
- Determiners precede the nouns.

FAQ 2: Are there any more cases where the adjectives can precede the noun?

Yes, in literature. Any alteration of the logical order of the sentence (called hyperbaton) reflects an emotional sense.

For example, in the verse "Volverán las oscuras golondrinas." * (The dark swallows will come back), the poet put the adjective before the noun to give it more relevance.

(*) *Rimas,* by Gustavo Adolfo Bécquer.

Exercises

Exercise 1

In the following sentences, write the adjective in parenthesis in the appropriate gender and number, and location among the options given underlined.

1. Las lámparas que me gustan son (luminoso)_____ , (azul) _____y (español)_____.

2. La penicilina fue un (grande)_____ avance para la Medicina.

3. María vive en el (primero) _____piso y yo en el (tercero)_____ piso.

4. María vive en la (primero) _____planta y yo en la (tercero) _____planta.

5. 99% es un (bueno) _____ resultado.

6. 99% es una (bueno) _____ calificación.

7. 40% es un (malo) _____ resultado.

8. 40% es una (malo) _____ calificación.

9. Mi (antiguo) _____carro_____ era un Ford, ahora tengo un Cadillac.

10. Pedro solo trabaja con (antiguo)_____ relojes_____, del siglo XIX o anteriores.

11. Los (bajo) _____ edificios_____ son más seguros cuando hay terremotos.

12. En la (bajo) _____Edad Media_____ es cuando se construyeron las grandes catedrales.

13. Antonio es un (grande) _____amigo_____, y siempre está dispuesto a ayudarme.

14. Antonio es un (grande)_____ hombre_____ : pesa como un toro.

15. El (medio) _____hombre_____ no aprende del pasado.

16. Tengo (medio) _____kilo_____ de caramelos.

17. Ana tiene el (mismo)_____ interés_____ que Lola en terminar el proyecto rápidamente.

18. Ana no sólo estudia Filosofía para obtener el titulo, ella tiene (mismo) _____interés_____ en la Filosofía.

19. Mi carro ya no funciona, necesito un (nuevo)_____ carro_____.

20. No me gustan los carros de segunda mano, me gustan los (nuevo) _____carros_____.

21. Es un (pobre)_____ hombre_____. Su salario es bajísimo.

22. Era un (pobre)_____ hombre_____ que gastaba su inmejorable salario en Las Vegas.

23. Es (puro) _____alcohol_____, 100% etanol.

24. Ese ron es (puro) _____alcohol_____,35% de alcohol.

25. En Sevilla, Antonio es mi (único) _____contacto_____.

26. Pérez-Reverte es un (único)_____ hombre_____: corresponsal de guerra, novelista y académico.

27. En Barcelona tengo un (viejo) _____amigo_____, Pedro, que trabaja con relojes.

28. A veces no vale la pena reparar los (viejo)_____ relojes_____.

29. (valiente) Los _____soldados_____ de Julio César desfilaron en Roma. Todos los del César.

30. (más valiente) Los _____soldados_____ sobrevivieron al ataque de los galos. Sólo 200 de los 6.000 hombres enviados.

Answers:

1. Las lámparas que me gustan son: luminosas, azules y españolas.
   The lamps I like are: bright, blue, and Spanish.

2. La penicilina fue un gran avance para la Medicina.
   Penicillin was a big breakthrough in Medicine.

3. María vive en el primer piso y yo en el tercer piso.
   María lives on the first floor and I live on the third floor.

4. María vive en la primera planta y yo en la tercera planta.
   Mary lives on the first floor and I live on the third floor.

5. 99% es un buen resultado.
   99% is a good result.

6. 99% es una buena calificación.
   99% is a good grade.

7. 40% es un mal resultado.
   40% is a bad result.

8. 40% es una mala calificación.
   40% is a bad grade.

9. Mi antiguo carro era un Ford, ahora tengo un Cadillac.
   My old car was a Ford, now I have a Cadillac.

10. Pedro solo trabaja con relojes antiguos, del siglo XIX o anteriores.
    Pedro only works with antique clocks, from the nineteenth century or earlier.

11. Los edificios bajos son más seguros cuando hay terremotos.
    The short buildings are safer when there are earthquakes.

12. En la baja Edad Media es cuando se construyeron las grandes catedrales.
    In the late Middle Ages is when they built the great cathedrals.

13. Antonio es un gran amigo, y siempre está dispuesto a ayudarme.
    Antonio is a great friend and he is always willing to help me.

14. Antonio es un hombre grande y pesa como un toro.
    Antonio is a big man and weighs as much as a bull.

15. El hombre medio no aprende del pasado.
    The average man does learn from the past.

16. Tengo medio kilo de carmelos.
    I have half a kilo of sweets.

17. Ana tiene el mismo interés que Lola en terminar el proyecto rápidamente.
    Ana has the same interest as Lola to finish the project quickly.

18. Ana no sólo estudia Filosofía para obtener el titulo, ella tiene interés mismo en la Filosofía.
    Ana not only studies Philosophy to obtain the diploma, she really has interest in Philosophy.

19. Mi carro ya no funciona, necesito un nuevo carro.
    My car is not working any more, I need a new car.

20. No me gustan los carros de segunda mano, me gustan los carros nuevos.
    I do not like second-hand cars, I like brand-new cars.

21. Es un hombre pobre. Su salario es bajísimo.
    He is a poor man. His salary is very low.

22. Era un pobre hombre que gastaba su inmejorable salario en Las Vegas.
    He was a poor man that spent his excellent salary in Las Vegas.

23. Es alcohol puro: 100% etanol.
    It is pure alcohol: 100% ethanol.

24. Ese ron es puro alcohol: 35% de alcohol.
    That rum is "pure" alcohol: 35% alcohol

25. En Sevilla, Antonio es mi único contato.
    In Seville, Antonio is my only contact.

26. Pérez-Reverte es un hombre único: corresponsal de guerra, novelista y
    académico.
    Perez-Reverte is a single man: war correspondent, novelist, and scholar.

27. En Barcelona tengo un viejo amigo, Pedro, que trabaja con relojes.
    In Barcelona I have an old friend, Peter, who works with clocks.

28. A veces no vale la pena reparar los relojes viejos.
    Sometimes it's not worth repairing old clocks.

29. Los valientes soldados de Julio Cesar desfilaron en Roma.Todos los del
    César.
    The brave soldiers of Julius Caesar marched on Rome. All Caesar's.

30. Solo los soldados valientes sobrevivieron al ataque de los galos. Solo 200
    de los 6000 hombres enviados.
    Only the brave soldiers survived the attack of the Gauls. Only 200 out of
    6000 men sent.

4. PRONOUNS
PRONOMBRES

Pronouns are those words that substitute a noun. Because of them, when the subject of the sentence is known, you avoid repeating the noun:

Mary said **Mary** bought **the car**, now **the car** is **Mary's.**
She   said **she**   bought **it,**   now **it**   is **hers.**

In English, they all are:

Personal pronouns	Possessive pronouns	Object pronouns	Reflexive pronouns
I	mine	me	myself
you	yours	you	yourself
he, she, it	his, hers, its	him, her, it	himself, herself, itself
we	ours	us	ourselves
you	yours	you	yourselves
they	theirs	them	themselves

←──────────────→ ←──────────────────→

Same position Spanish/English   Position can be different

We'll group the pronouns by types in four tables (each group corresponds to a column of the above table).

Personal Pronouns

Personal pronouns are the subject of the sentence. They are:

English	Spanish
I	yo
you	tú
he, she, it	él *, ella, ello
we	nosotros, nosotras
you guys (Spain)	vosotros, vosotras
you guys / they	ustedes/ ellos, ellas

> (*) Notice that él (= he) has an accent mark. This is to distinguish it
> from "el" (= the)

The personal pronouns are commonly placed before the verb, as in English.

> **Yo** trabajo mucho.
> **I** work a lot.

The use of these words in Spanish is very limited. Spanish doesn't use the
personal pronouns (I, you, he…) in normal speech. Instead, the information of
"who does" the action is carried by the verb's ending.

The personal pronoun is used to emphasize:

> **Yo** lo pagué (instead of: Lo pagué).
> "**I**" paid for that.

If you use the personal pronoun, it must go before the verb, with only two
optional exceptions: the imperative mood and questions.

Example:
> - Imperative mood:
>> Prepare it!
>> ¡Prepáralo **tú**! (more common)
>> ¡**Tú,** Prepáralo! (less common)

> - Questions:
>> Where do you study?
>> ¿Dónde estudias **tú**? (more common)
>> ¿**Tú** dónde estudias? (less common)

There are two extra personal pronouns. One is "usted," with the same meaning
of "tú" ("you" singular), and the other is its plural: "ustedes."

Golden Rule

There are two differences between **tú and usted**, as per their use:

"Tú" is the common and **in**formal way of treatment.
"Tú" is conjugated with its own verb forms (the forms of "tú" that appear in this book).

"Usted is used only to address someone very formally (like a stranger on the street or an official in court)
"Usted" **is conjugated with the verb forms of "'él/ella"**

There are two differences between **vosotros and ustedes**, as per their use:

"Vosotros" (used only in Spain) is the common and **in**formal way of treatment equivalent to "you guys."
"Vosotros" is conjugated with its own verb forms (the forms of "Vosotros" that appears in this book).

"Ustedes" **in Spain** is used only to address a group of people very formally (like strangers on the street or officials in court). **In Latin America**, "ustedes" doesn't make this distinction formal/informal. It simply means "you plural."
"Ustedes" **is conjugated with the verb forms of "ellos."**

Appendix A: Notes about Dialects shows the use of the pronouns according to the three main dialects. The following examples show some translations to the forms "tú,"and "usted":

> ¿Cómo te llamas (tú)?
> ¿Cómo se llama (usted)?
> What's your name?

> ¿Cuántos años tienes (tú)?
> ¿Cuántos años tiene (usted)?
> How old are you?

> ¿De dónde eres (tú)?
> ¿De dónde es (usted)?
> Where are you from?

> ¿Cuánto tiempo llevas (tú) aquí?
> ¿Cuánto tiempo lleva (usted) aquí?
> How long have you been here?

Possessive Pronouns

They indicate possession. They are:

English	Spanish
mine	mío, mía, míos, mías
yours	tuyo, tuya, tuyos, tuyas
his, hers, its	suyo, suya, suyos, suyas
ours	nuestro, nuestra, nuestros, nuestras
yours	vuestro, vuestra, vuestros, vuestras (Spain)
yours / theirs	suyo, suya, suyos, suyas

The possessive pronouns are placed in the sentence as in English.

Examples :

> Mi carro es gris. → El mío es gris. (carro is singular, masc.)
> My car is gray.   → Mine is gray.
>
> Mis tortugas son grises. → Las mías son grises. (plural, femin.)
> My turtles are gray.   → Mine are gray.

Unlike English, in Spanish you can precede the possessive pronoun with the article el/ la/ los/las. You can say: "Esta casa es la mía" (= This house is mine).

You will use the article when you are specifying a concrete element among a set:

> Esta casa es mía. Yo poseo esta casa.
> This house is mine. I own this house.
>
> Esta es una foto aerea del vecindario, esta casa es **la** mía.
> In this aerial photo of my neighborhood, this house is mine.

Object Pronouns

The object pronouns are those that receive the action. In "I see him," *I* is the subject and *him* the object.

The **English** object pronouns are:

me
you (singular)
him, her, it
us
you (plural)
them

Unlike English, in Spanish they can be classified, in turn, into five types of **pronouns**:

1. After a preposition different from "con" and "entre" (= with, between), e.g. "That gift is for **her**."
2. After the preposition "con" with" e.g. "He may go with **her**."
3. After the preposition "entre" between" e.g. "Between **you** and **me** there are no secrets.
4. Direct Object pronoun (D.O), e.g. "I have written **it**".
5. Indirect Object pronoun (I.O.), e.g. "I have written it to **her**".

The first three types of pronouns are placed in the sentence as in English.

> Ese documento es para **ella.**
> That document is for **her.**

However, the direct and indirect pronouns are not always placed as in English.

> **Lo** he visto.
> I have seen **it.**

> Voy a ver**lo.**
> I am going to see **it.**

Table of pronouns:

Type 1: pronouns after a preposition	Type 2: pron. after the prep. "con" (= with)	Type 3: pron. after the prep. "entre" (= between)	Type 4: Direct Object pronoun	Type 5: Indirect Object pronoun
mí	conmigo	yo	me	me
ti	contigo	tú	te	te
él, ella, ello	con él, ella, ello	él, ella, ello	lo, la	le (se)
nosotros/ as	con nosotros/ as	nosotros/ as	nos	nos
vosotros/ as (Spain)	con vosotros/ as (Spain)	vosotros/ as (Spain)	os (Spain)	os (Spain)
ustedes, ellos/ ellas	con ustedes, ellos/ ellas	ustedes, ellos/ ellas	los/ las	les (se)

Examples:

Ese documento es para **ella.**
That document is for **her.**

Voy a registrarme con **ella**.
I am going to register with **her.**

Entre **tú** y **yo** no hay secretos.
Between **you** and **me** there are no secrets.

La he visto.
I have seen **her**.

Le he dicho que eso es imposible.
I have told **her** that that is impossible.

Classification

Type 1. Pronouns with Prepositions different than "con" (= with), and "entre" (between)

The pronouns after prepositions (for, from, etc.) are placed in the sentence as in English.

Examples:
for me, by me, to me, from me...
para mí, por mí, a mí, de mí...

The pronouns with preposition are:

English	Spanish
me	mí
you	ti
him, her, it	él, ella, ello
us	nosotros, nosotras
you guys	vosotros, vosotras (Spain)
you guys / them	ustedes/ ellos, ellas

Notice that "mí" (= me) has an accent mark. This is to distinguish it from "mi" (= my). Also notice that the table looks like that of the Personal Pronouns, with the exception of "mí" and "ti."

Type 2. Pronouns with the preposition "con" (= with)

When the preposition is "con" (= with), the pronouns to use are the following:

English	Spanish
with me	conmigo *
with you	contigo *
with him, her, it	con él/con ella/ con ello
with us	con nosotros/con nosotras
with you guys	con vosotros/ con vosotras (Sp.)
with you guys/ with them	con ustedes/ con ellos, ellas

(*) Notice that "conmigo" is a single word, so is "contigo." Also notice that the table looks like that of the Personal Pronouns, with the exception of "conmigo" and "contigo."

Remember that the pronouns after prepositions are placed in the sentence as in English. Example:

> Pedro va a cantar con ella y contigo.
> Pedro is going to sing with her and with you.

Type 3. Pronouns with the preposition "entre" (between)

When the preposition is "entre" (= between, among), the pronouns to use are the following:

Spanish

yo
tú
él/ ella/ ello
nosotros/ nosotras
vosotros/ vosotras (Spain)
ustedes/ ellos, ellas

Notice that the table looks like that of the Personal Pronouns.

Remember that the pronouns after prepositions are placed in the sentence as in English. Example:

> Between you and me, that debate has no sense.
> Entre tú y yo, ese debate no tiene sentido.

Type 4. Direct Object (D.O.) pronouns

The Direct Object is the part of the sentence that respond to "what." In "I sing a song," what do I sing? The D.O. is "a song."

The D.O. pronouns are:

English	Spanish
me	me
you	te
him, her, it	lo, la
us	nos
you guys (Spain)	os
you guys / them	los, las

To translate "it" into Spanish, use "lo" if masculine, and "la" if feminine.

Example:
> **Lo** he visto (el libro).
> I have seen **it** (a book).

The preposition "a" (= to) precedes the D.O. when the following circumstances occur simultaneously: the D.O. is a person (versus an animal or a thing), and the name is not substituted by the pronoun.

> He visto **a** María.
> I have seen Maria.

> Estoy llamando a María ahora.
> I am calling Maria now.

But you may **not** use the preposition "a" in sentences as:

> La estoy llamando ahora.
> I am phoning **her** now.
>
> He visto **gatos** allí.
> I have seen **cats** there.

The pronoun "lo" is used with the verb "ser" or "estar" (to be) regarless of the gender or number of the object. For example:

> "Son ustedes María y Elena Pérez?" "Sí, **lo** somos"
> "Are you Mary and Luisa?" " Yes, we are."

In English, both the D.O. and the I.O. pronouns are always placed after the verb (e.g. I saw **them**). In Spanish, these pronouns commonly go before the verb. This bring us to another golden rule:

Golden Rule

> In Spanish, you can place the D.O. and the I.O. pronoun before the verb.
> This rule has three exceptions: 1) the imperative form, 2) the infinitive when not functioning as a verb, and 3) the gerund when not functioning as a verb.
> If the pronoun goes after the verb, it is written as part of the verb.

Example of the rule:

> El doctor **me** ha dicho que no estoy enfermo.
> The doctor has told **me** that I'm not sick.

These are all the possible cases:

- **La** vi.
  I saw **her** (single-verb form, not the imperative).

- (yo) **La** he visto.
  I have seen **her** (double-verb form with past participle).

- (él) **Lo** $\boxed{\text{va}}$ a $\boxed{\text{analizar}}$ en la oficina. Or:
  (él) $\boxed{\text{Va}}$ a analizarlo en la oficina. *
  He is going to analyze **it at the office** (double-$\boxed{\text{verb}}$
  structure with infinitive).

- (él) **Lo** está analizando en la oficina. Or:
  (él) Está analizán**dolo** en la oficina.*
  He $\boxed{\text{is}}$ $\boxed{\text{analyzing}}$ **it** at the office (double-$\boxed{\text{verb}}$ structure
  with gerund).

(*) Notice that you can opt to write the pronoun at the end
when you have a double-verb structure with infinitive or
with gerund.

Examples of the exceptions indicated in the golden rule above are:

- ¡Cántalo! (imperative form).
  Sing it!

- Después de ver**lo**, lo creo.
  After seeing it, I believe it (infinitive, here not
  functioning as a verb).

- Repitién**dolo**, lo memorizas (gerund, here not
      fuctioning as a verb).
  Repeating it, you memorize it.

Type 5. Indirect Object (I.O.) Pronouns

The Indirect Object (I.O.) answers "to whom?" In the sentence "I
said that to her," "that" is the D.O. , and "her" is the I.O.

The I.O. pronouns are:

English	Spanish
me	me
you	te
him, her, it	le (se)
us	nos
you guys (Spain)	os
you guys / them	les (se)

Notice that "le" and "les" are the only differences from the previous set of pronouns (the D.O. pronouns).

The placement of the I.O. follow the same golden rule of the D.O. pronouns.

The Indirect Object pronouns in Spanish can be repeated and you can have both the noun and its pronoun in the same sentence.

>Le he contado el secreto a ella ["le" is required]
>(Le) he contado el secreto a mi madre. ["le" is the common]
>I have told the secret to her/ to my mother.

The Direct Object pronouns can also be repeated but this is not so common.

>La vi a ella ayer. ["la" is required]
>La vi a tu madre ayer. ["la" is the common in some areas *]
>I saw her/ your mother.

>El periódico lo compra mi hijo todos los días
>My son buy the newspaper every day.

>(*) Very rarely found in Spain. Example: "A veces la odio a Elsa" -from Ramón J. Sender- (Sometimes I hate Elsa).

Use of D.O and I.O. in the same sentence

Golden Rule

> You can have two object pronouns together (e.g. "He said **it** to **us**"). In English and Spanish, the order is commonly the reverse. In Spanish, the I.O. pronoun goes first.
> In addition, you can have neither the combination "le lo," "le los" nor "le la", "le las." In these cases, you must substitute "le/les" for "**se**:" se lo, se la, se los, se las.

Example:

>**Nos lo** ha dicho. (nos = to us, lo = it)
>He has said **it** to **us.**

>Le lo he dicho → **Se lo** he dicho.
>I have said **it** to **him.**

Reflexive Pronouns

The reflexive pronouns are:

English	Spanish
myself	me
yourself	te
himself, herself, itself	se
ourselves	nos
yourselves (Spain)	os
yourselves/ themselves	se

Example:

Pedro **se** ha mirado en el espejo.
Pedro has looked at **himself** in the mirror.

Regarding the placement, the reflexive pronouns follow the same golden rule as the D.O. and I.O. pronouns, which is:

Golden Rule

In Spanish, you can place the reflexive pronoun before the verb.
This rule has three exceptions: 1) the imperative form, 2) the infinitive when not functioning as a verb, and 3) the gerund when not functioning as a verb.
If the pronoun goes after the verb, it is written as part of the verb.

Examples:

Él no **se** ha convencido de ello.
He hasn't convinced **himself** of it.

In Spanish, these pronouns are also used to express **reciprocity**: "one another" or "each other."

Peter y José **se** van a odiar.
Peter and José are going to hate **each other.**

Lucía, Marcos y yo **nos** hemos mirado.
Lucia, Marcos, and I have looked at **one another**.

A last comment about reflexive pronouns is the translation of sentences as: "I'll have my hair cut," "I'll have my car fixed" etc., which are reflexive in Spanish, even though the subject is not actually the barber or the mechanic:

> **Me** voy a cortar el pelo; **Me** voy a reparar el coche.
> I'm going to have my hair cut; I'm going to have my car repaired.

The pronoun with "ser" and "estar"

The pronoun that accompany the verb "ser" and "estar" (to be) is always "lo," regardless of the gender and number of the noun that the pronoun substitutes.

> ¿Estás casada, Lory? Lo estoy.[not *La estoy*]
> Are you married, Lory? I am.
>
> ¿Son ustedes las nuevas chicas de la fraternidad? Lo somos.
> Are you the new girls of the sorority? We are.

Relative Pronouns

The relative pronouns are another type of pronoun that substitute a subject that is a sentence. In the sentence:

> Mary is the member of the club <u>who</u> helped me with my admission.

This is equivalent to saying:

> Mary is member of the club. <u>Mary</u> helped me with my admission.

Above you can see that the pronoun "who" substitutes "Mary."

The English relative pronouns are: who, whom, what, that, whose, the one that, etc.

Don't forget that in Spanish, unlike English, you cannot omit the relative pronoun "que" (= that).

> Dudo que él venga
> I doubt (that) he comes.

We have to distinguish six types of sentences sorted by the kind of "antecedent," which is the noun that preceeds the pronoun.

1. Sentences without any antecedent

> Pedro es ⌈quien⌋ me ayudó.
> Pedro es ⌈el que⌋ me ayudó.

> Pedro is ⌈who⌋ helped me. (the word that precedes "who" is
> not a noun)

> Esa heramienta es ⌈lo que⌋ me ayudó.
> That tool is ⌈what⌋ helped me.

English	Spanish
who, the one that the ones that	quien, quienes el que, la que, los que, las que
what	lo que, los que, la que, las que

2. Sentences with antecedent, and no separation between antecedent and pronoun

> Esa es ⌈la mujer⌋ ⌈que⌋ me ayudó.
> That is ⌈the woman⌋ ⌈who⌋ helped me ("the woman" precedes
> the pronoun "who").

> Ese es ⌈el carro⌋ ⌈que⌋ la atropelló.
> That is ⌈the car⌋ ⌈that⌋ ran over her.

English	Spanish
who	que
that	que

3. Sentences with antecedent, and some separation between antecedent and pronoun, typically a one-syllable preposition between antecedent and pronoun

> Esa es ⌈la mujer⌋ con ⌈quien⌋ me fui al hospital.
> Esa es ⌈la mujer⌋ con ⌈la que⌋ me fui al hospital.
> That is ⌈the woman⌋ with ⌈whom⌋ I went to the hospital.

Ese es el martillo con el que me rompí la pierna.
That is the hammer with which I broke my leg.

English	Spanish
who, whom	quien, quienes, el que, la que , los que, las que
which	el que, la que , los que, las que

4. Sentences with antecedent, and longer separation between antecedent and pronoun, typically a multi-syllable preposition between antecedent and pronoun

Ese es el juez ante el cual presenté mi caso.
That is the judge before whom I presented my case.

Ese es el invento acerca del cual Pedro ha hablado tanto.
That is the invention about which Pedro has spoken so much.

English	Spanish
who, whom	el cual, la cual, los cuales, las cuales
which	el cual, la cual, los cuales, las cuales

5. Sentences with an antecedent which is a sentence

Antonio era el unico candidato con experiencia, lo que hizo su elección inmediata.
Antonio was the only candidate with experience, which made his election immediate.

English	Spanish
what	lo que
which	lo cual, lo que

6. Sentences with an antecedent which is a possessive.

Lucas, cuya hija se rompió un pierna, no vendrá este verano.
Lucas, whose daughter broke her leg, won't come this summer.

English	Spanish
whose	cuyo, cuya, cuyos, cuyas

Remember that "whose" when is in a question, is translated by "De quién"

¿De quién es este carro?
Whose car is this?

Frequently Asked Questions

FAQ1: Again, what's the direct object?

It is the part of the sentence over which the action of the verb falls. In the sentence, **He wrote a letter to Mary yesterday**, the Direct Object would be "a letter," since this is what "he" wrote.

In general, a complete clause follows the pattern:

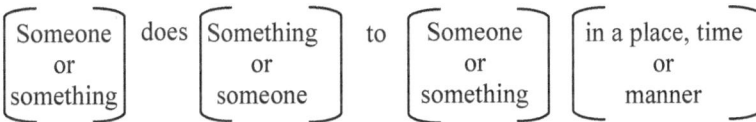

Someone or something	does	Something or someone	to	Someone or something	in a place, time or manner

Someone or something	(Subject)	He
does	(Verb)	wrote
Something or someone	(Direct Object)	a letter
to someone or something	(Indirect Object)	to Mary
in a time, place or manner	(Circumstantial Object)	yesterday

FAQ 2: I've heard that even native speakers confuse the words: "la, le, lo." Is there a rule of thumb?

Many native speakers confuse *la, le* and *lo* in certain occasions.

The rule of thumb that those speakers use is:

le or **lo**   for masculine
la   for feminine

FAQ 3: I've heard that in some cases, it is accepted to use "le" as a direct object pronoun too. How come?

It is accepted in Spanish, but it is recommended that you use the proper rule (*lo/la* for D.O., and *le* for I.O.). This question requires a deeper understanding of Spanish and a deeper explanation.

As we saw, there are two types of object pronouns: direct and indirect object pronouns (D.O. and I.O.). Roughly, direct pronouns respond to the question "what/who;" indirect pronouns respond to "to what/to whom?"

> I've written <u>a letter</u> to <u>the senate.</u>
> DIRECT   INDIRECT

> **What** have you written? A letter
> **To whom** have you written? **To** the senate

Spanish distinguishes the direct object from the indirect object for the following pronouns: la, le, lo, las, les, los. The others (me, te, nos) are invariable.

English	Spanish	
	D.O	I.O.
me	me	me
you	te	te
him	**lo**	**le**
her	**la**	**le**
it	**lo/la**	**le**
us	nos	nos
you guys (Spain)	os	os
you guys/ them	**los /las**	**les**

We can write:

	D.O.	I.O.
masculine	lo	le
feminine	la	

	D.O.	I.O.
masculine	los	les
feminine	las	

Examples:

> Sobre esas plantas de allí, ese jardinero **las** ha regado.

About the plants over there, that gardener has watered them.

El cartero **los** va a distribuir.
The mailman is going to distribute them [the parcels].

El cartero **les** va a poner etiquetas.
The mailman is going to put labels on them [the parcels].

The straightforward way to know if an object is direct or indirect is to change the sentence to passive voice. This will result in the subject of the sentence being the direct object.

The postman put **labels** on the packets.
Labels are put on the packets by the postman.

The use of "le" as a D.O. is accepted when the D.O. is a person and it is masculine.

	D.O.	I.O.
masculine	lo/le	le
feminine	la	

	D.O.	I.O.
masculine	los	les
feminine	las	

Le vi. (accepted) / Lo vi. (as per the norm)
I saw him

The tendency in many cases is to use a pattern that doesn't depend on D.O./I.O.

	D.O.	I.O.
masculine	le	
feminine	la	

	D.O.	I.O.
masculine	les	
feminine	las	

Vi el perro. Le vi. (popular use, although not correct)/ Lo vi. (as per the norm)
I saw the dof. I saw it.

Exercises

Exercise 1

Translate the following sentences (Note: translate "to say" as "decir")

1. [In Spain] You guys have to visit the Canary Islands in order to say that you know Spain.
2. [In Spain] I was telling you guys to come.
3. I saw her.
4. I do this to see her.
5. I've seen her.
6. I'm going to see her.
7. I can see her right now.
8. I will tell the secret to Mary tomorrow without fail.
9. Say that to her
10. You will need courage to say that to her.
11. I have said that to her
12. I am going to say that to her
13. I'm saying that to her now
14. I will say that to her tomorrow
15. This gift is for me.
16. Maria has decided that she is going to come with me.
17. There are no secrets between them and me.
18. Peter refuses to accept the truth.
19. I regret having resigned.
20. I fell in love with Cali: its music, food, people, etc..
21. I feel sorry for having said that her.
22. It is horrible that children of separated parents blame themselves for the separation.
23. Many abuses were committed against Mexicans during the bracero program.

Answers:

1. (Vosotros) Tenéis que visitar las Islas Canarias para poder decir que conocéis toda España.
2. Os estaba diciendo que vinierais.
3. La vi.
4. Hago esto para verla.
5. La he visto.
6. La voy a ver.
   Voy a verla.
7. La estoy viendo ahora mismo.
   Estoy viéndola ahora mismo.
8. Le diré el secreto a María mañana sin falta.
   Se lo diré mañana sin falta.
9. Díselo.
10. Necesitarás coraje para decírselo.

11. Se lo he dicho.
12. Se lo voy a decir.
    Voy a decírselo.
13. Estoy diciéndoselo ahora.
    Se lo estoy diciendo ahora.
14. Se lo diré (a ella) mañana.
15. Este regalo es para mí.
16. Maria ha decidido que va a venir conmigo.
17. No hay secretos entre ellos y yo.
18. Pedro se niega a aceptar la verdad.
19. Me arrepiento de haber renunciado.
20. Me enamoré de Cali: su música, su comida, su gente, etc.
21. Me siento mal por habérselo dicho.
22. Es horrible que los hijos de padres separados se culpen por la separación.
23. Muchos abusos se cometieron en contra de los mexicanos durante el programa bracero.
    Muchos abusos fueron cometidos en contra de los mexicanos durante el programa bracero.

Exercise 2

Rewrite the following sentences replacing the fragment underlined by an appropriate pronoun.

1. ¡Pásame la pelota!
   Pass me the ball!

2. Escribí una carta a Pedro, pero no me contestó.
   I wrote a letter to Pedro, but he did not answer me.

3. Voy a escribir una carta   a Pedro.
   I am going to write a letter to Pedro.

4. [España] Quiero contar una historia a Juanito y a ti que no olvidaréis.
   I want to tell a story to Juanito and you that you won't forget.

5. Con su alergia, Manuel está perdido si prueba esta zanahoria.
   With his allergies, Manuel is lost if he tries this carrot.

6. Voy a preguntar esas dudas   a Francisco.
   I'll ask those questions to Francisco.

7. Lucas y yo presentaremos los nuevos productos a los directores.
   Lucas and I will present the new products to the directors.

8. Pidió a Pedro y a mí   nuestro carro   para ese viaje.
   He asked Peter and me for our car for the trip

Answers:

1. ¡Pásame<u>la</u>!

2. <u>Le</u> escribí una carta, pero no me contestó.

3. Voy a escribír<u>sela</u>.
   <u>Se la</u> voy a escribir.

4. <u>Os</u> quiero contar una historia que no olvidaréis.
   Quiero contar<u>os</u> una historia que no olvidaréis.

5. Con su alergia, Manuel está perdido si <u>la</u> prueba.

6. Voy a preguntár<u>selas</u>.
   <u>Se las</u> voy a preguntar

7. <u>Nosotros se los</u> presentaremos.

8. <u>Nos lo</u> pidió para ese viaje.

Exercise 3

Translate the following sentences into Spanish putting special attention to the relative pronouns: que, cual, etc.

1. The documents that were saved in the fire will help in court.
2. I don't know anyone who speaks French better than Pierre.
3. Some people combat stressful times simply with loneliness.
4. The geese, that before visited us every year, now don't pass through here.
5. In general, people who weigh more can drink more alcohol without feeling its effects.
6. I earn very little and we could not live without what my wife earns.
7. There are countless schools in which students face uneven conditions.
8. I'm sure I have the necessary certification for the job.
9. Mary is who helped me.
10. Look at this newspaper: it raises things with which I completely agree.
11. Something similar Lenin said, for whom money was the sinews of war.
12. Citizens, many of whom do not vote ever, for some reason, did en masse yesterday.
13. The flu virus mutates very rapidly, which means that there is no permanent vaccine.
14. *Don Quixote* begins with: "In a village of La Mancha, whose name I do not want to remember / ... / ".
15. Whose pencil is this?
16. Peter, whose daughter was at the party, will not come.
17. This is the university in whose classrooms I studied.

Answers:

1. Los documentos que se salvaron en el incendio ayudarán en el juicio.
2. No conozco a nadie que hable francés mejor que Pierre.
3. Algunas personas combaten los tiempos de estrés con simple soledad.
4. Los gansos, que antes nos visitaban todos los años, ahora no pasan por aquí.
5. En general las personas que tienen más peso pueden beber más alcohol sin notar sus efectos.
6. Yo gano muy poco y no podríamos vivir sin lo que gana mi esposa.
7. Hay un sinfín de escuelas en las que los alumnos se enfrentan a condiciones desiguales.
8. Estoy segura de que tengo la certificación necesaria para ese trabajo.
9. María es quien (la que) me ayudó.
10. Mira este periódico: plantea cosas con las que estoy completamente de acuerdo.
11. Algo parecido decía Lenin, para quien (para el que) el dinero es el nervio de la guerra.
12. Los ciudadanos, muchos de los cuales no votan nunca, por alguna razón ayer lo hicieron en masa.
13. El virus de la gripe muta muy rápidamente, lo cual hace que no existan vacunas permanentes.
14. El Quijote empieza con: "En un lugar de La Mancha, de cuyo nombre no quiero acordarme/.../".
15. ¿De quién es este lápiz?
16. Pedro, cuya hija estaba en la fiesta, no vendrá.
17. Esta es la universidad en cuyas aulas yo estudié.

5.   PREPOSITIONS
PREPOSICIONES

The function of prepositions is to join parts within a sentence, unlike the conjunctions, which join sentences.

Álvaro is **from** Perú
　　　　 PREP.

Alvaro is from Perú and Lucas is from Chile
　SENTENCE 1　CONJ.　SENTENCE 2

Prepositions are: at, in, on, from, of, over, under, below, etc.

Some words can act as prepositions or adverbs (adverbs are words that respond to "how, when, where").

　　 I'm <u>inside</u> the house [Here "inside" links two elements].
　　　　 PREP.
　　 Estoy <u>dentro de</u> la casa.
　　　　　 PREP.

　　 I am <u>inside</u>. [Here "inside" responds to "where?"]
　　　　 ADV.
　　 Estoy <u>dentro.</u>
　　　　 ADV.

Multiple-word Prepositions

Multiple-word prepositions are expressions that function as a preposition. For example the three-word expression "on top of" is equivalent to the preposition "on."

Multiple-word expressions that function as prepositions are:

dentro de ...*	= inside ...
fuera de...	= outside...
alrededor de...	= around...
junto a...	= next to...
al lado de...	= side by side...
cerca de ...	= near, close to, circa, around...
lejos de ...	= far from...
en medio de...	= in the middle of...
al principio de...	= at/in the beginning of...
al final de...	= at/in the end of...
encima de...	= on top of...
debajo de...	= under...

(*) Ellipses points (...) are written to indicate that there must be some words afterwards. Otherwise, they would not be functioning as a preposition but as an adverb. Remember: an adverb answers where, when, or how.

I'm <u>inside</u> the house.
          PREP.
Estoy <u>dentro de</u> la casa.
          PREP.

I am <u>inside</u>.
          ADV.
Estoy <u>dentro.</u>
          ADV.

The "multiple-word propositions" are easy to study since they have a one-to-one translation in Spanish.

Single-word Prepositions

The Spanish prepositions (single word prepositions) are:

Spanish	English
a *	to, at
ante	before
bajo	under, below
con	with
contra	against
de *	of, from, off
desde	from
durante	during
en *	in, on, at
entre	between, among
hacia	to, towards
hasta	until, up to
mediante	by means of, by
para *	for, to
por *	for, by, to
según	according to
sin	without
sobre	on, over, above
tras	after
vía	via
versus	versus

(*) These prepositions are explained in detail later in this chapter.

Examples:

Voy a clase **a** las 3.
I go to class **at** 3 o'clock.

Le dije a John" hola" muchas veces, pero no me respondió.
I said "hi" to John many times, but he didn't responded to me.

Ha hablado **ante** el juez.
He has spoken **before** the judge.

El gato está **bajo** la mesa.
The cat is **under** the table.

La temperatura es **bajo** cero.
The temperature is **below** zero.

Es el hermano **de** María.
He's María**'s** brother (Spanish doesn't have this structure).

He llegado aquí **de** Canadá.
I have arrived here **from** Canada.

Es un anuncio **de** Coca Cola.
It's a Coca-Cola ad.

Voy a estudiar **desde** las 3.
I am going to study **from** 3 o'clock.

Peter ha navegado **desde** Cuba.
Peter has sailed **from** Cuba.

Voy a escribir mis memorias **durante** el verano.
I am going to write my memoirs **during** summertime.

Voy a comer **en** una hora.
I am going to eat **in** one hour.

He vivido **en** Los Ángeles.
I have lived **in** Los Angeles.

El tres está **entre** el 2 y el 4.
Three is **between** 2 and 4.

Juan está **entre** la multitud.
Juan is **among** the crowd.

Está caminando **hacia** la puerta.
He is walking **to** (towards) the door.

Voy a estudiar **hasta** las 3.
I am going to study **until** 3 o'clock.

Peter ha navegado **hasta** Cuba.
Peter has sailed **up to** Cuba.

Voy a escribir mis memorias **durante** el verano.
I am going to write my memoirs **during** summertime.

Mediante esa técnica, he destruido todos los gérmenes.
By this technique, I have destroyed all germs.

El martillo es **para** martillear.
A hammer is **for** hammering.

¿**Para** aquí o **para** llevar?
For here or **to** go?

Estoy yendo allí **por** una razón.
I am going there **for** one reason.

Ha sido devorado **por** un león.
He has been devoured **by** a lion.

Está bailando **sobre** el tejado.
He is dancing **on** the roof.

Su avión va a volar **sobre** la ciudad.
His plane is going to fly **over** the city.

Ha corrido **tras** él.
He has run **after** him.

Tras el incidente, ha declarado.
After the incident, he has declared.

Voy a enviar mi solicitud **vía** *email.*
I am sending my application **via** email.

Ese conflict, Roma **versus** Cartago, fue una guerra mundial.
That conflict, Rome **versus** Carthage, is considered a world war.

This chapter will analyze those Spanish prepositions that admit more than one translation.

1. *A* (= to)

In Spanish, when the Direct Object is a person, then the D.O. is preceded by the preposition "a." This use is called the personal "a" (*la "a" personal*). Examples:

> He visto **a** María en el baile.
> I have seen Maria at the ball.

Ha abrazado **a** mi padre.
He has embraced my father.

He admirado Madrid y he admirado **a** Picasso.
I have admired Madrid and I have admired Picasso.

The exception of the rule is when the person is abstract, as in: "Estamos buscando el mejor candidato" (We are looking for the best candidate).

2. *De* (= of)

Unlike English, Spanish doesn't have the structure called Saxon genitive: Peter**'s** house; the cat**'s** basket.

However, Spanish uses the same alternative that English has, the preposition "of" (de).

La casa **de** Pedro; la cesta **del** gato
The house **of** Peter; the basket **of** the cat

3. *En* (= in, on, at)

In many cases "en" is translated not only by "in," but also by "on," "at."

El lápiz está **en** el cajón.
The pencil is **in** the drawer.

El libro está en la mesa. Está trabajando **en** el hospital.
The book is on the table. She is working **at** the hospital.

Súbete **en** el autobús.
Get **on** the bus.

4. *Para / Por* (= to, for, by)

The translation of "for" can be either "para" or "por." A first approach to distinguish them is the following:

- "Para" expresses: purpose or use
- "Por" expresses: means, cause, or passive voice

Examples:

Trabajo **para** IBM.
I work **for** IBM [It expresses a purpose].

Para clavar eso, vas a necesitar un martillo.
For nailing that, you are going to need a hammer [purpose].

Para clavar eso, vas a necesitar un martillo.
To nail that you are going to need a hammer [a purpose].

Gracias **por** cantar.
Thank you **for** singing [a cause].

Enviaré este paquete **por** UPS.
I will send this parcel **by** UPS. [a means].

Me regañó **por** llegar tarde.
He scolded **for** being late [a cause].

No tienes luz **por** no pagar la factura de la electricidad.
You don't have power **because** you didn't pay the bill [a cause].

El ladrón fue cogido **por** la policía.
The thief was caught **by** the police [passive voice].

Examples of expressions with prepositions not matching in Spanish and English.

English	Spanish
Juan is from Los Angeles	Juan es **de** Los Angeles
to write **by** hand	escribir **a** mano
meat **on** the grill	Carne **a** la parrilla
about 7 o'clock	**hacia** las siete
It's covered **with** snow	Está cubierto **de** nieve
The girl **with** the red shirt	La chica **de** la camisa roja
It's one block **from** here	Está **a** un bloque de aquí
on Tuesday	el martes
on October 2, 2007	el 2 de octubre de 2007
2 hours **ago**	**hace** 2 horas
for two hours	dos horas

Prepositions associated with verbs

Unlike English, Spanish does not have verbs having a preposition as an intrinsic part of it.

> Cancelé mi cita.
> I called **off** my appointment.

Don't confuse this concept with the fact that some verbs have an associated proposition. For example the verb "to depend" can have a preposition or not (so it's not a phrasal verb) but when the verb is followed by a phrase, this phrase needs the preposition "on." Spanish has also this feature.

> Eso depende.
> This depends.[no preposition]
>
> Eso depende **de** su exactitud.
> This depends **on** its accuracy.

The preposition "on" is not an intrinsec part of the verb "to depend" since you can say "It depends" , with no preposition.

It is common that dictionaries include the preposition that are associated with each verb, for example:

Spanish	English
depender (de)	to depend (on)
constar (de)	to consist (of)
pensar (en)	to think (of)
soñar (con)	to dream (about)
insistir (en)	to insist (on)
contar (con)	to rely (on)

Prepositions Replaced by an Adjective

Unlike English, Spanish can't normally substitute a preposition by an adjective.

> Esta es una compañía de Coca Cola.
> This one is a Coca Cola company. [Here Coca Cola is a noun
>   functioning as an adjective].
> This is a company **of** Coca Cola.
>
> Pedro es un conductor **de** Texas.

Pedro is a Texas driver.
Pedro is a driver **from** Texas.

Esas muestras fueron enviadas **por** correo
Those samples were mail delivered
Those samples were delivered **by** mail.

The saxon's genitive is a similar structure with two nouns, the owner and the owned using an apostrophe on the owned, as in "Juan's house." This structure doesn't exist in Spanish. Spanish uses the preposition "de."

La casa de Juan es esa.
Juan's house is that one.
The house **of** Juan is that one.

Frequently Asked Questions

FAQ 1: Is it correct to write two prepositions together?

The Spanish grammar only accepts rare cases where one preposition introduces a prepositional group. For example, you can say:

Caminé **por** la pared rota.[where broken wall = pared rota]
I walked though the broken wall.

But if you substitute the name for an expression that is already introduced by a preposition, you can also say:

Caminé **por entre** los árboles.
I walked through the woods. [Consider: woods = entre los árboles]

A very common combination in Spain is "a por":

Voy a por agua.
I fetch water.

FAQ 2: What is "queísmo" and "dequeísmo"?

Queísmo is the wrong use of "que" instead of "de que."

~~Me di cuenta que no tenía dinero.~~
Me di cuenta de que no tenía dinero.
I realized that I didn't have money

Dequeísmo is the wrong use of "de que" instead of "que.

Pienso de que debes ir. [wrong]
Pienso que debes ir. [right]
I think you must go.

Examples of correct sentences:

Pienso algo	→ pienso **que**.. .(= I think that...
Opino algo	→ opino **que**... (It is my opinion that...)
Dudo de algo	→ dudo **de que**... (I doubt that...)
Estoy seguro de algo	→ estoy seguro **de que**... (I am sure that...)
Aviso de algo	→ aviso **de que**... (I warn that...)

FAQ 3: Can I say "alrededor mío," since "mío" means "de mí"?

Yes, you can. The reason is because you can use a preposition before "alrededor," as "a mi alrededor.
However, you can't say "delante mío," for you can't say: "en mi delante" or "de mi delante," or "delante" with any preposition preceding it.

Exercises

Complete the following sentences with the appropriate preposition.

1. Pienso _____ eso todos los días.

   I think about that every day.

2. Eso depende _____ ella.

   That depends on her.

3. La caja está _____ese armario.

   The box is on top of that cabinet.

4. Los hombres de la mudanza no dejarán las cajas _____ el pasillo.

The movers will not leave the boxes in the middle of the corridor.

5. Tiró la pelota _____ la ventana.

He threw the ball at the window.

6. Claudia fue _____ Madrid _____ estudiar _____ la universidad.

Claudia went to Madrid to study at the university.

7. Hay una farmacia _____ un bloque de aquí.

There's a pharmacy one block from our house.

8. La carta está escrita _____ mano.

The letter is written by hand.

9. Esta mañana vi _____ tu tío.

This morning I saw your uncle.

10. Están buscando _____ una nueva sirvienta.

We are looking for a new maid.

11. ¿Por qué no vienes _____ las siete?

Why don't you come about seven o'clock?

12. Pasaron la mañana entera _____ el mercado.

They spent the entire morning at the market.

13. La casa _____ mi hermano es muy fría.

My brother's house is very cold.

14. Kazumi es _____ Japón.

Kazumi is from Japan.

15. Las montañas estaban cubiertas _____ nieve.

The mountains were covered with snow.

16. La mujer _____ el sombrero gris es mi prima.

The woman with the gray hat is my cousin.

17. Ellos le quitaron el juguete _____ el niño.

They took the toy away from the child.

18. _____ la muerte de su esposa, está siempre triste.

Since his wife's death, he has always (been) sad.

19. _____ trabajar allí, necesitas un permiso especial.

To work there you need a special permit.

20. Pedro trabaja _____ IBM.

Pedro works for IBM.

21. Envío todos mis paquetes _____ UPS.

I send all my parcels by UPS.

22. ¿Tú caminas _____ todas las salas cuado visitas un museo?

Do you walk around all the rooms when you visit a museum?

23. Esa herramienta es _____ golpear.

That tool is for hammering.

24. No tenemos luz _____ no pagar la factura de la luz.

We don't have power because you didn't pay the bill.

25. Trabajé allí _____ dos años.

I worked there for two years.

Answers:

1. Pienso en eso todos los días.

2. Eso depende de ella.

3. La caja está encima de ese armario.

4. Los hombres de la mudanza no dejarán las cajas en medio del pasillo.

5. Tiró la pelota a la ventana.

6. Claudia fue a Madrid a estudiar a la universidad.

7. Hay una farmacia a un bloque de aquí.

8. La carta está escrita a mano.

9. Esta mañana vi a tu tío.

10. Están buscando una nueva sirvienta.

11. ¿Por qué no vienes sobre/ hacia las siete?

12. Pasaron la mañana entera en el mercado.

13. La casa de mi hermano es muy fría.

14. Kazumi es de Japón.

15. Las montañas estaban cubiertas de nieve.

16. La mujer del sombrero gris es mi prima.

17. Ellos le quitaron el juguete al niño.

18. Desde la muerte de su esposa, está siempre triste.

19. Para trabajar allí, necesitas un permiso especial.

20. Pedro trabaja para IBM.

21. Envío todos mis paquetes por UPS.

22. ¿Tú caminas por todas las salas cuado visitas un museo?

23. Esa herramienta es para golpear.

24. No tenemos luz por no pagar la factura de la luz.

25. Trabajé allí (durante) dos años.

6. SUBJUNCTIVE
EL SUBJUNTIVO

Verb tenses can be classified into: indicative, subjunctive and imperative.
They are called "modes."

- **Indicative** gives information objectively. Thus, in the sentence:

   Manuel viene hoy.
   Manuel comes today [where "comes," is indicative].

   the speaker expresses the event "Manuel comes today" as a fact,
   with no emotion, no doubt, etc.

- **Subjunctive** gives information subjectively. Thus, in the
   sentence:

   Espero que Manuel venga hoy.
   I hope that Manuel come today. ["come" is subjuctive].

   The speaker expresses the event "Manuel comes today" not as a
   fact, but with emotion: with hope.

- **Imperative** expresses commands. As in:

   Manuel, ven.
   Manuel, come.

The infinitive, gerund and past participle (to sing, singing and sung) don't fit in this classification. These three forms (called the non personals forms of the verb) can't function as a verb by themselves. They become part of a indicative or subjunctive sentence depending on other verbal form that they accompany. For example. The sentence "I sung yesterday." is incorrect. "Sung" can only work in combination with other verbal forms, such as "have sung" to render an indicative or a subjective sentence:

> Has cantado bien.
> You have sung well [indicative].

> Es importante que hayas cantado bien en la entrevista.
> It is important that you have sung well in the interview [subj.].

Below you can see the table of Spanish verbal tenses using the example verb "cantar:"

	Simple tenses		**Compound tenses**	
Indicative Mood				
• Present	canto	I sing	he cantado	I have sung
• Preterite	canté	I sang	-	
• Imperfect	cantaba	I sang	habia cantado	I had sung
• Future	cantaré	I'll sing	habré cantado	I'll have sung
• Conditional	cantaría	I'd sing	habría cantado	I'd have sung
Subjunctive Mood				
• Present	cante	I sing	haya cantado	I have sung
• Past	cantara	I sang	hubera cantado	I had sung
Imperative Mood				
• Imperative	¡Canta!	Sing!	-	

Notes: 1. The table doesn't include the impersonal forms: infinitive (= to sing), gerund (= singing) and past participle (= sung).
2. The English form for the subjunctive coincide with the indicative.

English has Subjuctive but it is rarely used. It comes to light when it substitutes the indicative form. For example, when the subject is the third person singular (he, she, or it) in the present tense, or when the verb is "to be:"

> Espero que Manuel venga hoy.
> I hope that Manuel come today.

where "come" substitutes "comes," which would be the present tense (of indicative). Another example is:

> Si yo <u>fuera</u> rico, compraría ese violín.
> If I <u>were</u> a rich man, I would buy that violin. ["were" substitutes "was"].

The differentiation between indicative and subjunctive is not frequent in English; in addition, the speakers commonly use the indicative form in subjunctive sentences:

> If I <u>was</u> a rich man, I would buy that violin.
> I hope that Manuel <u>comes</u> today.

The Subjunctive Tenses

In order to master the use of the Spanish subjunctive, you need to get familiar with the conjugations of the four subjunctive tenses.

The table of **the subjunctive tenses** for the regular verbs are:

	AR Verbs	ER Verbs	IR Verbs
Simple Present Subjunctive			
(I)	-e *	-a	-a
(you singular)	-es	-as	-as
(he/she/it)	-e	-a	-a
(we)	-emos	-amos	-amos
(you guys) - Spain-	-éis	-áis	-áis
(you guys/ they)	-en	-an	-an

	AR Verbs	ER Verbs	IR Verbs
Simple Past Subjunctive			
(I)	-ara	-iera	-iera
(you singular)	-aras	-ieras	-ieras
(he/she/it)	-ara	-iera	-iera
(we)	-áramos	-iéramos	-iéramos
(you guys) - Spain-	-arais	-iérais	-iérais
(you guys/ they)	-aran	-ieran	-ieran

Compound Present Subjunctive

(I)	haya	-ado	haya	-ido	haya	-ido
(you singular)	hayas	-ado	hayas	-ido	hayas	-ido
(he/she/it)	haya	-ado	haya	-ido	haya	-ido
(we)	hayamos	-ado	hayamos	-ido	hayamos	-ido
(you guys) - Spain-	hayáis	-ado	hayáis	-ido	hayáis	-ido
(you guys/ they)	hayan	-ado	hayan	-ido	hayan	-ido

Compound Past Subjunctive

(I)	hubiera	-ado	hubiera	-ido	hubiera	-ido
(you singular)	hubieras	-ado	hubieras	-ido	hubieras	-ido
(he/she/it)	hubiera	-ado	hubiera	-ido	hubiera	-ido
(we)	Hubiéramos	-ado	hubiéramos	-ido	hubiéramos	-ido
(you guys) - Spain-	hubierais	-ado	hubierais	-ido	hubierais	-ido
(you guys/ they)	hubieran	-ado	hubieran	-ido	hubieran	-ido

(*) Dash indicates that it is an ending. For example: the forms of the verb
     "cantar" would be: cante, cantes, etc.; cantara, cantaras, etc.; haya
     cantado, hayas cantado, etc.; hubiera cantado, hubieras cantado, etc.

There are two additional forms, one for the Simple Past Subjunctive, and one
for the Compound Past Subjunctive. **These two extra forms are called the
forms in "SE"** because they are the result of substituting "RA" for "SE".

Table of subjunctive forms in "SE":

	AR Verbs	ER Verbs	IR Verbs

Simple Past Subjunctive

	AR Verbs	ER Verbs	IR Verbs
(I)	-ase	-iese	-iese
(you singular)	-ases	-ieses	-ieses
(he/she/it)	-ase	-iese	-iese
(we)	-ásemos	-iésemos	-iésemos
(you guys) - Spain-	-aseis	-iéseis	-iéseis
(you guys/ they)	-asen	-iesen	-iesen

Compound Past Subjunctive

(I)	hubiese	-ado	hubiese	-ido	hubiese	-ido
(you singular)	hubieses	-ado	hubieses	-ido	hubieses	-ido
(he/she/it)	hubiese	-ado	hubiese	-ido	hubiese	-ido
(we)	hubiésemos	-ado	hubiésemos	-ido	hubiésemos	-ido
(you guys) - Spain-	hubieseis	-ado	hubieseis	-ido	hubieseis	-ido
(you guys/ they)	hubiesen	-ado	hubiesen	-ido	hubiesen	-ido

In Latin America the forms in RA are of common use, and the forms in SE are used only in literature; however in Spain both forms (in RA and in SE) are used with the same frequency.

There exists a future subjunctive but is not in use any longer. You only can see this tense in non contemporary literature and in judicial documents. You can obtain the future subjunctive by replacing the last "a" for an "e" in the tenses of the past subjunctive. Thus, the future subjunctive of cantar would be: cantare, cantares, etc.; and the compound future subjunctive would be: hubiere cantado, hubieres cantado, etc.

Regarding the conjugations of the present and past subjunctive of the irreguar verb, in the book *Spanish for Californians: Using English to Learn Spanish,* you can find an extensive classification of the irregularities:

- Present Subjunctive: there are spelling-changing or false-irregular verbs, and five types of irregular verbs (the same as the present tense).
- Past Subjunctive: there are five types of irregular verbs (the same as the preterite tense).

Grammatical Instances of Subjunctive

With a brief grammatical analysis, you can limit greatly the cases where the subjunctive is to be used instead of the indicative.

In order to do that, we need to define the concepts: verb structure, main and subordinate clause, and simple and compound sentence.

- A **verb structure** is a set of verbs that act as one verb in a sentence. For example:

    I sang yesterday [one verb: to sing].

    I have to sing now [two verbs: to have and to sing].

    I am letting him go [three verbs: to be, to let, and to go].

- A **sentence** is the grammatical unit that ends with a full stop or !?

    A sentence can have more than one verb structure, e.g.

    I am suggesting that he comes . [two verbal structures]

- **A clause** is a fragment of a sentence that has one and only one verb structure.

  Clauses can be classified into: **main clause**, when it is independent; and **subordinate clause**, when it is dependent of other clauses in the sentence.

- **A simple sentence** is a sentence with only one clause (only one verb structure) e.g. "I <u>am letting him go</u>."

  A non-simple sentence has two or more verb structures, e.g. " I am suggesting that he comes."

  There are two types of compound sentences:

     - A compound (or coordinate) sentence, which has two or more main clauses, e.g.

       <u>I don't come</u>   but   <u>he comes.</u>
         MAIN CLAUSE   MAIN CLAUSE

       The link in a coordinate sentence is a conjunction as: and, or, but, so.

     - A complex sentences has one main, and one or more subordinate clauses, e.g.

       <u>I am suggesting</u> that <u>he comes.</u>
         MAIN CLAUSE   SUBORDINATE CLAUSE

       The link in a complex sentence is a conjunction as: "that" or "if."

Conditions of existence of subjunctive:

Condition 1: Subjunctive can only be found in **non-simple sentences**, not in simple sentences.

There is one real exception: certain sentences of request, such as:

I'd like to see that dress of your shop window.
Quisiera ver ese vestido del escaparate.

There are two pseudo exceptions:

- The imperative form.

> Vayamos al cine.
> Let's go to the movie theatre.

This sentence looks like the subjunctive and it is a simple sentence; however it is not subjunctive. Some forms of the Imperative are identical to the Present Subjunctive.

Imperative	Pres. Subjunctive
-	cante
¡Canta (tú)!	cantes
¡Que cante (él/ella)! *	cante
¡Cantemos (nosotros)! *	cantemos
¡Cantad (vosotros)!-Sp.	canteis -Spain-
¡Canten (ustedes)! *	canten
¡Que canten (ellos)!*	

> (*) Notice that in these forms the imperative is identical to the present subjunctive.

- Sentences with words such as: quizás (= maybe), tal vez (= maybe) , ojalá (= I wish), probablemente (= probably), etc.

Each of those words is equivalent to a whole clause by itself, so a sentence with any of those words is not really a simple sentence.

> Es posible **que vaya**.
> Posiblemente/ Quizás/ Tal vez vaya.
> It is possible that I go.

> Es probable **que vaya**
> **Probablemente vaya**.
> It is probable that I go.

> Deseo **que vaya**.
> Ojalá **vaya**.
> I wish that he goes.

Condition 2: Subjunctive can only be found in **complex sentences**, never in compound sentences (coordinate sentences).

Condition 3: Subjunctive can only be found **in the subordinate clause**, never in the main clause.

This condition has one exception, the construction:

Compound Present Subjunctive + Compound Pres. Subjunctive
               MAIN   +   SUBORDINATE

Lo hubiera pintado si me lo hubieras pedido.
I would have painted it, if you had asked me.

Condition 4: Subjunctive can only be found **in sentences that express subjectivity**: possibility, doubt, emotion, etc.

The following diagram describes the portion of possible subjunctive clauses in the total of clauses.

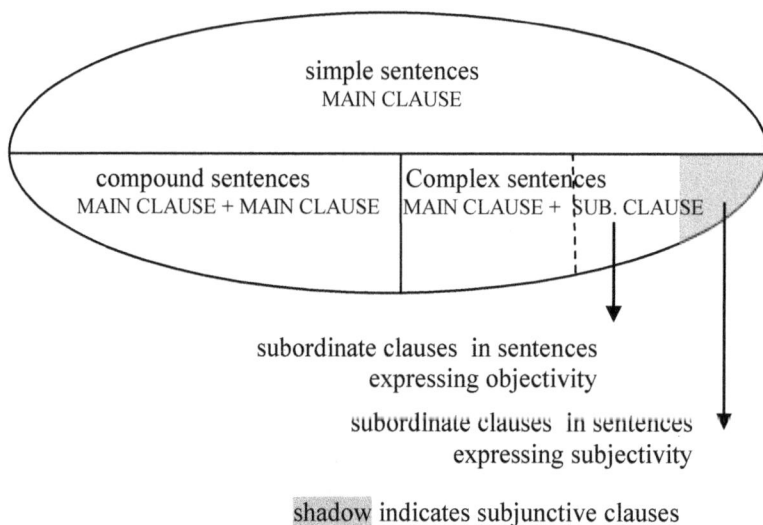

simple sentences
MAIN CLAUSE

compound sentences   Complex sentences
MAIN CLAUSE + MAIN CLAUSE   MAIN CLAUSE + SUB. CLAUSE

subordinate clauses in sentences
expressing objectivity

subordinate clauses in sentences
expressing subjectivity

shadow indicates subjunctive clauses

The oval above supposes to contain all sentences you can build in Spanish. The upper half would contain all simple sentences (sentences with just one clause). The lower left quadrant includes all coordinate sentences (sentences with main clauses). The lower right quadrant has all the complex sentences (sentences with a main and a subordinate clause) but only the subordinate clause of that area can have subjunctive verb tenses, and out of this portion, only those sentences that express wish, doubt, possibility, etc.

It is because of these limitations that the following **rule of thumb** can be used:

Commonly, a subjunctive tense is used after the word "que" (= that) when the sentence expresses: wish, doubt, possibility, and emotion.

It is a good exercise that you check the examples in this book and the number of times the subjunctive is following "que." Out of all examples of next section (Contextual Instances of Subjunctive), only the ones in "Case 5" the subjunctive tense is not following the word "que." This is the case of the words: *si* (= if), *cuando* (= when), *mientras* (= as long as), *en cuanto* (= as soon as).

Contextual Instances of Subjunctive

As said before, other than some grammar conditions (conditions 1, 2, and 3 above), the clause will be in subjunctive only if the sentence expresses a subjective context.

The subordinate clause will be in a subjunctive tense in the following cases:

Cases	Example	Translation
1. Desire	Quiero que...	I want ...
2. Probability	Tal vez...	Maybe...
3. Doubt	Dudo que...	I doubt that...
4. Emotion	Temo que...	I am afraid that...
5. Condition	Si...	If...
6. Goal	Para que...	In order that...
7. Impersonal	Es lógico que..	It's logical that...
8. Negative	No he oído que...	I haven't heard that...

Cases:

1. When the main sentence expresses **desire**. Examples:

Quiero que él venga.	I want him to come.
Ojalá que él venga.	I wish that he comes.
Busco que él venga.	I pursue that he comes.
Ruego que él venga.	I beg that he comes.
Ordeno que él venga.	I command that he comes.
Aconsejo que él venga.	I advise that he comes.
Tengo ganas de que él venga.	I'd like him to come.
Sugiero que él venga.	I suggest that he comes.
Prohíbo que él venga.	I forbid that he comes.
Me opongo a que él venga.	I am against that he comes.
Niego que él venga.	I deny that he comes.
Espero que él venga.	I hope that he comes.

2. When the main sentence expresses **probability**. Examples:

Es posible que él venga.	It's possible that he comes.
Es probable que él venga.	It's probable that he comes.
Es difícil que él venga.	It's hard for him to come.
Tal vez él venga.	Maybe he comes.
Quizá(s) él venga.	Maybe he comes.
Puede que él venga.	It's possible that he comes.

3. When the main sentence expresses **doubt**. Examples:

Dudo que él venga.	I doubt that he is coming.
No es evidente que él venga.	It's not evident that he is coming.
No creo que él venga.	I don't believe that he is coming.

However, expressions as *No dudo que* (I don't doubt that...), *Creo que* (= I believe that...), and *Es evidente que* (= It is evident that...) don't go with subjunctive since they don't express doubt but certainty or a fact.

No dudo que él viene.	I don't doubt that he comes.
Creo que viene.[indicative]	I believe he comes.
Es evidente que él viene [ind.]	It's evident that he comes.

4. When the main sentence expresses **emotion**. Examples:

Me sorprende que él venga.	I am surprised that he comes.
Temo que él venga.	I am afraid that he comes.
Me entristece que él venga.	I am sad that he comes.
Siento que él venga.	I feel sorry that he comes.
Me alegro de que él venga.	I am glad that he comes.

5. When the subordinate clause precedes the adverbial phases that implies a **condition and an expression of doubt** of the condition occurring. With the word "si" (=if), subjunctive expresses an unlkely situation. Examples:

Si *[a] vinieras, te compraría el regalo. [unlikely]	If you came, I'd buy the present.
Cuando *[b] vengas, te daré un beso.	When you come, I'll give you a kiss.
Mientras *[c] vengas, estaré contento.	As long as you come, I will be happy.

En cuanto *[d] vengas, lo escribiremos.	As soon as you come, we'll write it.
Hasta que *[e] vengas, no saldremos.	Until you come, we won't leave.
Antes de que *[f] vengas, habré terminado.	Before you come, I will have finished.
Después de que *[g] vengas, lo pensaremos.	After he comes, we'll think about it.
Aunque *[h] venga, no será suficiente.	Although he comes, it won't be enough.
Con que tú vengas, es suficiente.	As long as you come, I will be sufficient.
En caso de que vengas, lo preguntaré.	In case that you come, I will ask the question.
A menos que vengas, pediré ayuda.	Unless you come, I will ask for help.
Como si fuera otra persona, se comportó	As if he was another person, he behaved.
Sin que sirva de precedente, lo haré.	Without setting a precedent, I will do it.
Basta que ella venga, para que él se ponga contenta.	It suffices that she comes so that he is happy.

(*) Notice that sometimes the adverb can imply a condition that is not doubtful and it will not be subjunctive:

[a] Si vienes, te compro el regalo. [likely]	If you come, I'd buy you the present.
Si vienes, te compraré el regalo. [likely]	If you come, I will buy you the present.
Si vienes, ¡compra el regalo! [likely]	If you come, buy the present!
[b] Cuando vienes, te doy un beso.	(Every time) When you come, I give you a kiss.
[c] Mientras vienes, prepararé la cena.	While you are on your way, I will prepare the dinner.
[d] En cuanto vienes, todo se desorganiza.	Every time, as soon as you come, it's all a mess.
[e] Hasta que vienes, no salimos.	Every time, until you come, we don't leave.
[f] Antes de que vienes, termino.	Every time, before you come, I finish.
[g] Después de que vienes, lo hacemos	Every time, after you come, we do it.
[h] Aunque viene, no es suficiente.	Although he comes, it is not enough.

6. When the sentence expresses a goal and the subject of the main clause is different from that of the subordinate clause. Examples:

(yo) Trabajo duro para que (tú) vayas a la universidad.	I work hard so that you can go to college.
(yo) Trabajo duro a fin de que (tú) vayas a la universidad.	I work hard so that you can go to college.

7. In impersonal sentences with the verb *ser* (= to be). Examples:

Es lógico que tengas tantos problemas.	It's logical that you have so many problems.
Es importante que vengas puntual.	It is important for you to be on time.

8. In adjective clauses and direct object clauses, within negative sentences

An adjective clause is a clause that works as an adjective, in other words, that describe a noun. For example, in "I like old cars," "old" is the adjective; in "I like cars that were made before 1960," the ending "that were made before 1960", works as an adjective.

Likewise a D.O. clause works as D.O. in a complex sentence. For example, in "I have heard that he comes," " that he comes" is the D.O.

No hay nadie que venga hoy.	There is nobody that may come today.
No he oído que él venga.	I haven't heard that he is going to come.

Those sentences of above would be in indicative if they were positive:

Hay alguien que viene hoy.	There is somebody that comes today.
He oído que él viene.	I have heard that he is going to come.

Use of the Four Tenses of Subjunctive

Once you know that the verb tense must be subjunctive, you need to know which tense to use out of the four tenses:

- Present Subjunctive, e.g. cante
- Past Subjunctive, e.g. cantara
- Compound Present Subjunctive, e.g. haya cantado
- Compound Past Subjunctive, e.g. hubiera cantado

There is a golden rule inspired by Fred F. Jehle (Indiana University IPFW) to choose the right tense. First, the following terms must be defined:

Present time tenses include the present and future tense, both simple and compound and both indicative and subjunctive, and the imperative. So, it includes the tenses: "canto," "he cantado," "cantaré," "habré cantado, " "cante," "haya cantado," and "¡canta!"

Past time tenses include the conditional and past tenses, (preterite and imperfect), both simple and compound and both indicative and subjunctive. So, it includes the tenses: "cantaría," "habría cantado," "canté," "cantaba," "había cantado," "cantara," and "hubiera cantado."

Golden Rule

> **Use the present subjunctive** (simple or compound), when the verb of the main clause is in a "present time tense."
> **Use the past subjunctive** (simple or compound), when the verb of the main clause is in a "past time tense."
> **Use the simple** form of the subjunctive to express a simultaneous or future action.
> **Use the compound** form of the subjunctive to express a previous activity.

The English compound tenses correspond well with the Spanish counterparts. Thus, in the cases which you would use a compound tense in English (as "...that I have sung," or "...that I had sung"), use the Spanish equivalent ("...que haya cantado," or "...que hubiera cantado").

Thus:

> No me <u>importa</u> que **<u>haya sacado</u>** una baja puntuación.
> PRES. TIME TENSE   PRES. TIME TENSE
>
> I don't care that he **has scored** low.

No me <u>habría importado</u> que **<u>hubiera sacado</u>** una baja puntuación.
PAST TIME TENSE   PAST TIME TENSE

I wouldn't have care that he **had scored** low.

Exceptions and special cases

- Occasionally the verb in the main clause can refer to a present action, and the verb is referred to an action in the past.

  No <u>creo</u> que él <u>hubiera cometido</u> ese ese error cuando era joven.
  PRESENTE   PAST

  I doubt that he had made that mistake when he was young.

- When the Spanish subjunctive is translated in English by "may" or "might," the Spanish forms will be: present and past subjunctive, respectively. Past subjunctive indicates lower probability that the action occurs.

  Es posible que venga hoy. =He may come today.
  Es posible que **viniera** hoy. = He **might** come today.

  Llámame si tienes alguna pregunta. = Call me if you have any questions.
  Llámame si **tuvieras** alguna pregunta. = Call me if **you happen to**
  have any questions.

- The expression "como si" (= as if) is always followed by a **past** subjunctive.

  Él habla como si **hubiera vivido** en México.
  He talks as if he has (had) lived in Mexico.

- If the main clause has no verb, as "ojalá (= I hope) or "quizá" (=Perhaps), the actual meaning determines the one among the four tenses of subjunctive.

  Ojalá que él esté allí. = I hope he's there.
  Ojalá que él haya estado allí. = I hope he's been there.
  Ojalá que él estuviera allí. = I wish he were there.
  Ojalá que él hubiera estado allí. = I wish he had been there.

List of examples of subjunctive

- A main clause with a simple tense in the subordinate clause

Le estoy pidiendo a Carlos que **venga** hoy.
   MAIN CLAUSE   SUBORDINATE CLAUSE
I am asking Carlos to come today.

Es posible que Felipe **venga** hoy.
   MAIN CL.   SUB. CLAUSE
[OR: Puede que Felipe venga hoy.]
Felipe may come today.

Mañana le pediré a Carlos que **venga** a la reunión el próximo mes.
   MAIN CLAUSE   SUBORDINATE CLAUSE
Tomorrow I'll tell Carlos to come to the meeting next month.

Ayer te dije que **vinieras** bien preparado hoy.
   MAIN CL.   SUBORDINATE CLAUSE
I told you to come well prepared today.

Antes de la interrupción, te estaba diciendo que **vinieras** aquí.
                              MAIN CLAUSE   SUB. CLAUSE
Before the interruption, I was telling you to come here.

Te diría que **vinieras**, pero sé que no puedes.
MAIN CL.   SUB. CL.
I would tell you to come, but I know you can't.

Llámame si **tuvieras** alguna pregunta.
   MAIN CL.   SUBORDINATE CLAUSE
Call me if you had any questions.

Le he dicho a Carlos que **venga** aquí.
   MAIN CLAUSE   SUB. CLAUSE
I've told Carlos to come here.

Mañana a esta hora, le habré pedido que se **case** conmigo.
   MAIN CLAUSE   SUB. CLAUSE
Tomorrow at this time, I will have asked her to marry me.

Ayer, antes de la interrupción, te había dicho que **vinieras** a verme.
   MAIN CLAUSE   SUB. CLAUSE
Yesterday, before the interruption, I had told you to come see me.

- A main clause with a compound tense in the subordinate clause

> <u>No podré creer nunca</u> que <u>Juanito **haya escrito** tal cosa.</u>
> MAIN CLAUSE   SUBORDINATE CLAUSE
> I shall never be able to believe he has written such a thing.

> <u>Yo no podía creer</u> que <u>Juanito **hubiera escrito** tal cosa.</u>
> MAIN CLAUSE   SUBORDINATE CLAUSE
> I couldn't believe Juanito had written such thing.

> <u>Yo le habría dicho eso a Pedro</u> si <u>él **hubiera venido.**</u>
> MAIN CLAUSE   SUBORDINATE CLAUSE
> I would have said that to Pedro if he had come.

> <u>Yo no **hubiera creído** nunca</u> que <u>Juanito **hubiera escrito** eso.</u>
> MAIN CLAUSE   SUBORDINATE CLAUSE
> I would never have been able to believe Juanito had written such thing.

- Sentences with more than one main or subordinate clause

> <u>No veo a Vicente</u>, pero <u>no creo</u> que <u>**haya venido** antes del desayuno.</u>
> MAIN CL.1   M.CL.2   SUBORDINATE CLAUSE 2
> I don't see Vicente, but I don't believe has come before breakfast.
> ←——————→ ←————————————→

> <u>Yo no creía</u> que <u>Vicente **hubiera venido**</u> si <u>no se lo **hubiera pedido.**</u>
> MAIN CL.1   SUB.CLAUSE 1   SUB.CLAUSE 2
> I didn't believe Vicente had come   if I hadn't asked him.
> ←——————————→ ←————————→

> <u>Te habría dicho</u> que <u>**vinieras,**</u> si <u>**hubiera sabido** que te interesaba.</u>
> MAIN CLAUSE   SUB.CL.   SUBORDINATE CLAUSE
> I would have told you to come, if I had known you were interested.
> ←——————————→ ←————————→

> <u>Te **hubiera dicho*** que **vinieras,** si **hubiera sabido** que te interesaba.</u>
> MAIN CLAUSE   SUB.CL.   SUBORDINATE CLAUSE
> I would have told you to come, if I had known you were interested.
> ←——————————→ ←————————→

Frequently Asked Questions

FAQ: I still confuse indicative and subjunctive, can the native speakers really understand me?

Yes, they can; however subjunctive is a day-to-day feature of Spanish. Every native speaker uses it.

Exercises

Translate the following sentences into Spanish with the appropriate verb tense in indicative or subjunctive mood.

1. En condiciones normales de presión, el agua (hervir) _____ a 100 grados centígrados.
   Under normal pressure, water boils at 100 degrees Celsius.

2. La televisión no funciona porque la antena (estar) _____ rota.
   The television does not work because the antenna is broken.

3. Hoy precisamente (querer)_____ que ustedes (ir)__.
   Just today I want you to go.

4. Yo (querer)_____ (ir)_____.
   I want to go.

5. Ojalá que yo (conseguir)__ _____ el trabajo.
   I wish I get the job.

6. Ojalá que Pedro (conseguir)_____ el trabajo.
   I wish Pedro gets the job.

7. Juan (buscar)_____alguien que le (ayudar)____ _con su página web.
   Juan looks for someone to help her with her website.

8. Manuel (buscar)_____un trabajo urgentemente.
   Manuel looks for a job urgently.

9. Te (rogar)_____ que me (acompañar)_____a esa fiesta.
   I beg you to accompany me to that party.

10. Ayer el general (ordenar)_____ que todo el regimiento (salir)_____a las ocho.
    Yesterday, the general ordered the to leave at eight.

11. Nuestros hijos ya (ordenar)_____ los juguetes solos.
    Our children already sort their toys alone.

12. Los médicos (aconsejar)_____ que se (dormir)_____ la siesta.
    Doctors advise that people nap.

13. Los médicos (aconsejar)_____(dormir)_____ la siesta.
    Doctors advise taking a nap.

14. Yo (tener)_____ganas de que (llegar)_____ las vacaciones.
    I'm looking forward to the holidays arriving.

15. Yo (sugerir)_____que nosotros (usar)_____más tiempo en
    esta parte del proyecto.
    I suggest that we use more time in this part of the project.

16. Yo (sugerir)_____ (usar)_____ más tiempo en esta parte del proyecto.
    I suggest using more time in this part of the project.

17. No (sugerir)_____que el país (tener)_____ que (prohibir)_____el uso
    de PVC.
    I don't suggest that the country has to ban the use of PVC.

18. El director se (oponer)_____ a que los niños (caminar)____solos al colegio.
    The principal objects that the children walk to school alone.

19. El director (negar)____ que la mayoría de los niños (caminar)_____al
    colegio solos.
    The director denies that most of the children walk to school alone.

20. Yo (esperar)_____ que tú (conseguir)_____el trabajo.
    I hope you get the job

21. Yo (esperar) _____el tren cinco minutos más y (volver)____ a casa.
    I wait for the train five more minutes and go home.

22. (Ser)_____ posible una solución negociada.
    It is possible a negotiated solution.

23. Es probable que ellos (llegar)_____ .
    It is likely that they arrive.

24. (Ser)_____ difícil que España y Reino Unido se (poner)_____ de acuerdo
    en eso hoy.
    It is difficult for Spain and the UK agree on that today.

25. Va a ser difícil para España y Reino Unido (poner)_____ se de acuerdo
    en eso.
    It is going to be easy for Spain and the UK to agree on that.

26. Yo tal vez lo (comprar)_____, si te tocara la lotería, querida.
I might buy it if you win the lottery, my dear.

27. Yo quizás lo (comprar)_____ hoy porque ya tengo el dinero.
Maybe I purchase it today because I have the money already.

28. Yo puede que lo (comprar)_____ .
I may purchase it.

29. Yo pudiera ser que lo (comprar) _____.
I might buy it.

30. No es evidente que los dos se (conocer)_____
It is not evident that they know each other.

31. Es evidente que los dos se (conocer)_____
It is evident that they know each other.

32. Yo no (creer)_____ que Esteban (tener)_____ razón.
I do not think Esteban is right.

33. Yo (creer)_____ que Esteban (tener)_____ razón.
I do believe that Esteban is right.

34. Me (sorprender)_____que el conflicto no (haber) ____ escalado.
I'm surprised the conflict hasn't spiraled up.

35. Yo (temer)_____que ese medicamento esté perjudicándole.
I fear that the drug is hurting him.

36. ¿Te alegra o te entristece que Juan (querer)_____a María?
Are you happy or sad that Juan loves Maria?

37. Después de mi operación quirúrgica, siento que mis nervios
    (responder)_____como antes.
After my surgery, I feel my nerves respond as before.

38. Siento que el gato (haber)_____ muerto.
I feel sorry that the cat has died.

39. Si el dado (salir)_____1,2 o 3, te lo (dar)_____ .
If the die shows 1,2 or 3, I will give it to you.

40. Si tú (ganar)_____la lotería , te lo (dar)_____ .
If you win the lottery, I'd give it to you.

41. Todos los días, cuando me (despertar)_____ llamo a mi novia.
Every day when I wake up, I call my girlfriend.

42. Mañana, cuando me (despertar)____ llamaré a mi novia para decírselo.
Tomorrow when I wake up, I call my girlfriend to tell her.

43. Mientras yo (cocinar)_____, veo la televisión.
    While I cook, watch TV.

44. Mientras yo (cocinar)_____ tú tienes que seguir mis instrucciones en la
    cocina.
    While I cook, you have to follow my instructions in the kitchen.

45. En cuanto Manuel (llegar)_____, le daremos el regalo de cumpleaños.
    As Manuel arrived, we will give him the birthday present.

46. En cuanto mi esposa (llegar)_____, le doy un beso.
    As soon as my wife comes, I give her a kiss.

47. Hasta que Pedro (tener)_____ 18 años, no puede votar en España.
    Until Pedro is 18, he can not vote in Spain.

48. Aquí, todos los años, hasta que (llegar)_____ el invierno, no se ve nieve.
    Here, every year, until winter arrives, snow is not seen.

49. Manolito, antes de que yo (regresar)_____, tienes que ordenar todos tus
    juguetes.
    Manolito, before I return, you must order all your toys.

50. Manolito, después de que yo (regresar)_____ , haremos tu tarea del colegio.
    Manolito, after I return, we will do your homework.

51. En Fin de Año, después de que la gente se (ir)_____ de fiesta, toma el
    chocolate con churros.
    At New Year, after parting, people go take the chocolate with churros.

52. Cariño, con que tú (cocinar)_____ dos veces a la semana, me conformo.
    Honey, as long as you do the kitchen twice a week, I settle for it

53. A menos que las clases (ser)_____ muy caras, me apuntaré.
    Unless classes are very expensive, I will sign up.

54. Esa noche, comió como si no (haber)_____ comido nunca.
    That night, he ate as if he had ever eaten.

55. La compañía de seguros AAA hará todos los trámites, sin que tú
    (tener)_____que venir.
    The AAA insurance company will do all the paperwork, without you having
    to come.

56. Yo trabajo duro para que un día tú (ir)_____ a la universidad.
    I work hard so that one day you go to college.

57. Es lógico que ellos (cerrar)_____ la piscina con este frío.
    It is logical that they close the pool with this cold.

58. Es importante que tú (llegar)_____puntual a la
      entrevista.
    It is important for you to be punctual to the interview.

59. No he oído que el examen de conducir allí (ser)_____ difícil.
    I have heard that the driving test there is difficult.

60. No hay nadie que (estar)_____ seguro de eso.
    There is no one who is sure of that.

Answers:

1.   En condiciones normales de presión, el agua HIERVE (indicative) a 100
       grados centígrados.
2.   La televisión no funciona porque la antena ESTÁ (indicative) rota.
3.   Hoy precisamente yo QUIERO (indicative) que ustedes VAYAN
       (subjunctive).
4.   Yo QUIERO (indicative) IR.
5.   Ojalá que yo CONSIGA (subjunctive) el trabajo.
6.   Ojalá que Pedro CONSIGA (subjunctive) el trabajo.
7.   Juan BUSCA (indicative) alguien que le AYUDE (subjunctive) con su
       página web.
8.   Manuel BUSCA (indicative) un trabajo urgentemente.
9.   Te RUEGO (indicative) que me ACOMPAÑES (subjunctive) a esa fiesta.
10. Ayer el general ORDENÓ (indicative) que todo el regimiento SALIERA
       (subjunctive) a las ocho.
11. Nuestros hijos ya ORDENAN (indicative) los juguetes solos.
12. Los médicos ACONSEJAN (indicative) que se DUERMA(subjunctive) la
       siesta.
13. Los médicos ACONSEJAN (indicative) DORMIR la siesta.
14. Yo TENGO ganas de que LLEGUEN (subjunctive) las vacaciones.
15. Yo SUGIERO (indicative) que nosotros USEMOS (subjunctive) más
       tiempo en esta parte del proyecto.
16. Yo SUGIERO (indicative) USAR más tiempo en esta parte del proyecto.
17. No SUGIERO (indicative) que el país TENGA (subjunctive) que prohibir el
       uso de PVC.
18. El director se OPONE (indicative) a que los niños CAMINEN (subjunctive)
       solos al colegio.
19. El director NIEGA (indicative)que la mayoría de los niños CAMINEN
       (subjunctive) al colegio solos.
20. Yo ESPERO (indicative)que CONSIGAS (subjunctive) el trabajo.
21. Yo ESPERO (indicative)el tren cinco minutos más y VUELVO (indicative) a
       casa.
22. ES (indicative) posible una solución negociada.
23. Es probable que ellos LLEGUEN (subjunctive) .
24. ES (indicative) difícil que España y Reino Unido se PONGAN (subjunctive)
       de acuerdo en eso.

25. VA (indicative) A SER difícil para España y Reino Unido PONERSE de acuerdo en eso.
26. Yo tal vez lo COMPRARÍA (indicative), si te tocara (subjunctive) la lotería.
27. Yo quizás lo COMPRE (subjunctive) hoy porque ya tengo el dinero.
28. Yo puede que lo COMPRE (subjunctive).
29. Yo pudiera ser que lo COMPRARA (subjunctive).
30. No es evidente que los dos se CONOZCAN (subjunctive).
31. Es evidente que los dos se CONOCEN (indicative) .
32. Yo no CREO (indicative) que Esteban TENGA (subjunctive) razón.
33. Yo CREO (indicative) que Esteban TIENE (indicative) razón.
34. Me SORPRENDE (indicative)que el conflicto no HAYA (subjunctive) escalado.
35. Yo TEMO (indicative) que ese medicamento esté perjudicándole.
36. ¿Te alegra o te entristece que Juan QUIERA (subjunctive) a Maria?
37. Después de mi operación quirúrgica, siento que mis nervios RESPONDEN (indicative) como antes.
38. Siento que el gato HAYA (subjunctive) muerto.
39. Si el dado SALE (indicative)1,2 o 3, te lo DOY (indicative).
40. Si tú GANARAS (subjunctive) la lotería, te lo DARÍA (indicative).
41. Todos los días, cuando me DESPIERTO (indicative), llamo a mi novia.
42. Mañana, cuando me DESPIERTE (subjunctive), llamaré a mi novia para decírselo.
43. Mientras yo COCINO (indicative), veo la televisión.
44. Mientras yo COCINE (subjunctive), tú tienes que seguir mis instrucciones en la cocina.
45. En cuanto Manuel LLEGUE (subjunctive), le daremos el regalo de cumpleaños.
46. En cuanto mi esposa LLEGA (indicative), le doy un beso.
47. Hasta que Pedro TENGA (subjunctive)18 años, no puede votar en España.
48. Aquí, todos los años, hasta que LLEGA el invierno, no se ve nieve.
49. Manolito, antes de que yo REGRESE (subjunctive), tienes que ordenar todos tus juguetes.
50. Manolito, después de que yo REGRESE (subjunctive), haremos tu tarea del colegio.
51. En Fin de Año, después de que la gente se VA (indicative) de fiesta, toma el chocolate con churros.
52. Cariño, con que tú COCINES (subjunctive) dos veces a la semana, me conformo.
53. A menos que las clases SEAN (subjunctive) muy caras, me apuntaré.
54. Esa noche, comió como si no HUBIERA (subjunctive) comido nunca.
55. La compañía de seguros AAA hará todos los trámites, sin que tú TENGAS (subjunctive) que venir.
56. Yo trabajo duro para que un día tú VAYAS (subjunctive) a la universidad.
57. Es lógico que ellos CIERREN (subjunctive) la piscina con este frío.
58. Es importante que LLEGUES (subjunctive) puntual a la entrevista.
59. No he oído que el examen de conducir allí SEA (subjunctive) difícil.
60. No hay nadie que ESTÉ (subjunctive) seguro de eso.

7. OTHER CONSIDERATIONS ON VERBS
OTRAS CONSIDERACIONES SOBRE VERBOS

In addition to the use of subjunctive tenses, Spanish shows other grammatical elements which are foreign to the English speaker and commonly become an obstacle in learning. These are:

- Infinitive and Gerund (to sing vs. singing)
- Preterite and Imperfect Past (I sang vs. I used to sing)
- The verbs *Ser* and *Estar* (the verb *to be*)

Infinitive and Gerund

The infinitive is the proxy of the verb. In Spanish the infinitive always ends with AR, ER, IR (e.g. cantar, beber, vivir); in English the infinitive is preceded by "to" (to sing, to drink, to live), with some exceptions as "can," "may," etc.

The gerund in Spanish always ends in "ANDO," or "IENDO" (e.g. cantando, bebiendo, viviendo). In English the gerund ends in ING (e.g. singing, drinking, living). In English some verbs don't have a gerund: can, may.

Both the infinitive and the gerund are non personal forms of the verb, which means that these forms can't be conjugated: you can't say "yo cantar"(= I to sing) or "yo cantando" (= I singing). Thus, they must always work with an auxiliary verb. For example in "Voy a cantar" (= I am going to sing), it goes with the verb "ir" (= to go); and in "Estoy cantando" (= I am singing), it goes with the verb estar (= to be).

Periphrases are two verbs together in the same verb structure. There are two main types of periphrases: those where the second verb is in the infinitive form (with or without "to"); and those where the second verb is in the gerund form (with or without any preposition).

It's important that as you learn verbs (such as "to help," "can," "to start," "to avoid"), you learn which form to use for the second verb (either infinitive or gerund). In most of the cases Spanish and English coincide.

> (él) **Puede trabajar** duro cuando quiere.
> He **can work** hard when he wants.

But not always:

> Por favor, **evita usar** esta habitación (not ~~Evita usando~~).
> Please, **avoid using** this room.

Don't confuse periphrases with compound tenses. In the compound tenses (I have sung, I was singing" etc.), the first verb is an auxiliary verb whose only function is to create the tense. For example in the sentences: "I have to study;" "I am studying," the verb is "to study," the others (to have and to be) don't provide any meaning, only structure.

The verb "to want" forms periphrases in English, but does not in Spanish.

> Quiero que vayas (literally: "I want that you go").
> I **want** you to go.

The English infinitive (preceded by "to" or not) and the gerund don't coincide with their Spanish counterparts when using verbs as: can, may, to help, to start, to stop, to avoid, to like, to love, to look forward.

> Puede **trabajar** duro cuando quiere [infinitive "trabajar"].
> He can **work** hard when he wants [infinitive "to work" without "to"].

> Por favor ayúdame **a buscar** mi anillo [infinitive "buscar" with "a"].
> Please, help me **find** my ring [infinitive "to find" without "to"].

> Comencé **a estudiar** medicina [infinitive "estudiar" with "a"].
> I **started studying** medicine [gerund "studying"].

> Dejé **de estudiar** medicina [infinitive "estudiar" with "de"].
> I **stopped studying** medicine [gerund "studying"]

> Evita **usar** ese cuarto [infinitive "usar"]
> Avoid **using** this room [gerund "using"]

Me gusta/ me encanta **ver** películas [infinitive "ver"].
I like/ love **seeing** movies [gerund "seeing"].

Espero **conocerte** [infinitive "conocer"].
I look forward **to meeting** you [gerund "meeting" with "to"].

Another use of the Spanish infinitive is as a noun. In theory, every verb gives rise to a noun just by using its infinitive. For example, the verb "trabajar" (= to work) functions as a noun in:

El* <u>Cantar</u> me <u>atrae.</u> (= Singing appeals to me).
    NOUN   VERB

El* <u>Trabajar</u> <u>es</u> mi adicción (= Working is my addiction).
    NOUN   VERB

(*) When working as a noun, the article "el" is optional (never "la").

Notice in the examples above that English uses the gerund (or ING-words) instead of the infinitive for that structure.

The equivalent of: "(In order) to + INFINITIVE is: "Para + INFINITIVE"

Para tener mejores resultados necesitas estudiar más duro.
(In order) To have better results, you need to study harder.

The equivalent of: "For + GERUND is: "Para + INFINITIVE"

El martillo es **para martillear.**
The hammer is **for hammering**

In general, the equivalent of:

PREPOSITION DIFFERENT FROM "TO" + GERUND

is in Spanish:

PREPOSITION DIFFERENT FROM "A" + INFINITIVE.

Example:

Sin trabajar duro, no construirás tu reputación.

<u>**Without**</u>   <u>**working**</u> hard you won't build your reputation.
PREPOSITION   GERUND
DIFFERENT
FROM "TO"

Another use of the gerund is as an adverb. Most verbs give rise to adverbs just by using their gerunds. For example, the form "corriendo" (= running) functions as an adverb in:

> (yo) Llegué allí corriendo (I got there running)
> NOUN VERB   ADVERB

since "corriendo" answers the question "how?" How did you get there? Running.

Regarding irregularities in these two forms, Spanish has no irregular verb in the infinitive, and four types of irregular verbs in the gerund (They are analyzed in detail in the textbook *Spanish for Californians*).

Preterite and Imperfect Past

The English past tense "I sang" corresponds with two tenses in Spanish.

> **Canté** esa canción cinco veces y cada vez que la **cantaba**, lloraba.
> **I sang** that song five times and every time that **I sang** it I cried.

The second use of the past tense "I sang" is equivalent to "I was singing." We can state that:

Golden Rule

> If you can't substitute the past tense with the structure "I was singing" or "I used to sing," then it is the Preterite (versus the Imperfect Past tense).

> En 1939 Gran Bretaña **declaró** la guera a Alemania.
> In 1939 Great Britain **declared** war on Germany.

> En 1939 Gran Bretaña ~~declaraba~~ la guera a Alemania.
> In 1939 Britain ~~was declaring/used to declare~~ war on Germany.

In other cases, when it's clear that you mean an action with some duration or frequency, you don't have a choice.

> Cuando **estaba** en el colegio, **cantaba** en el coro.
> When I **was** at school, I **sang** in the choir.

Notice that the sentence "when I was at school" equals "when I was being a student." Example:

> Ayer **fui** a dar un paseo, como de costumbre. Cuando yo **estaba** en medio de mi camino, vi un perro. No le **presté** atención en ese momento, pero pronto me **di** cuenta que el perro me **seguía**. El perro **era** muy viejo, pero me **seguía** a mi ritmo. En ese momento en mi vida yo **corría** rápido. Cuando **llegué** a mi calle, el perro también **llegó**. El perro **entró** en mi casa de un vecino. Más tarde, mi vecino me dijo que su perro **era** muy independiente, pero nunca **iba** a dar un paseo "solo."

> Yesterday **I went** for a walk, as usual. When I **was** in the middle of my walk, I **saw** a dog. I **didn't pay** attention at that moment, but soon I **realized** the dog **followed** me. The dog **was** very old but **followed** my pace. At that time in my life I **ran** fast. When I **arrived** back to my street, the dog **did** too. The dog **came in** my neighbor's house. Later my neighbor said that his dog **was** very independent but he never **went** for a walk "on its own."

Ser and *Estar* (= to be)

As "to be," both *ser* and *estar* can work as an auxiliary verb and as a main verb (a verb carrying meaning).

> El ladrón fue detenido [ser].
> The thief was detained. [This is the passive voice. Here "to be" is an auxiliary verb; the main verb is "to detain"].

> Estoy visitando a mis padres ahora [estar].
> I am visiting my parents now [Here "to be" is an auxiliary verb; the main verb is "to visit"].

> Soy listo.
> I am smart [Here "to be" is the only verb; "smart" is an adjective].

> Estoy enfermo.
> I am sick. [Here "to be" is the only verb; "sick" is an adjective]

As an auxiliary verb, "to be" is easily translated by "ser" or "estar" since it has the same uses in Spanish.

- The passive voice (vs. active voice) always uses "ser" en Spanish

El pueblo fue reconstruido en un año, Or more commonly
El pueblo se reconstruyó en un año
The village was reconstructed in one year [passive voice]

Ellos reconstruyeron el pueblo en un año
They reconstructed the village in one year [active voice]

- Continuous tenses (as I am singing, I was singing, I will be singing, etc.) always use "estar" in Spanish

    Estoy trabajando en eso.
    I am working on that.

The problem is to chose "ser" or "estar" when they act as main verbs. When this happens, **to be** is translated by 1. SER, 2. ESTAR, 3. TENER or 4. HACER, as follows:

1. **SER** is used when the situation is permanent. The adjectives involved talk about the subject's identity.

    Es peruano. Es de Perú.
    He is Peruvian. He is from Peru. *[a]

    Es Juan.
    It's Juan.

    Es muy nervioso.
    He is a very nervous person.*[b]

    Pedro es delgado.
    Pedro is thin. [He is a thin person]*[c]

    Trabajar en una mina es sucio
    Working in a mine is dirty. *[d]

    Es agotador.
    He is tiring.

    (*) These examples are related to their counterparts below using "estar."

When the sentence includes a noun, *ser* is used because this implies a feature of the identity.

    Es una <u>persona</u> delgada.
    He is a thin <u>person</u>.
                 NOUN

Es un borracho.
He is a drunk.["drunk" is here a noun because of the article "a"]

Es una profesión sucia.
It's is a dirty profession.

Es un examen duro.
This is a hard exam.

2.   **ESTAR** is used when the situation is temporary (conveying the idea of where the subject is or how the subject looks like)

Está en Perú. *[a]
He is in Peru.

Está enfermo, loco, borracho.
He is sick, crazy, drunk.

Está nervioso por su examen.*[b]
He is nervous because of his exam.

Está delgado. *[c]
He is thin these days [He looks thin].

Está sucio después de trabajar en la mina. *[d]
He is dirty after working is the mine.

Está cansado.
He is tired.

(*) These examples are related to their counterparts above using "ser."

Past participles (e.g. forgotten, broken, proven, tired, prepared, etc.) can work as adjectives. When this happens they are translated always by "estar." This is because the past participle implies a temporary state.

Está cansado.[cansado is the past participle of "cansar"]
He is tired.[tired is the past parciple of the verb "to tire"]

Exceptionally the past participle can represent a permanent state, but even in this case, "estar" must be used, not "ser."

Esta muerto.["muerto" is the past participle of "morir"]
He is dead.

El poema está terminado con ese verso. ["terminado" is the past
                                  participle of "terminar"]
The poem is finished with that verse.

ANDAR (which literally means "to walk") can substitute *estar* when the
situation is temporary:

Anda enfermo/ nervioso/ en Perú/ cansado
He is sick/ nervous/ in Perú/ tired

Está muerto. El poema está terminado con ese verso.
~~Anda muerto. El poema anda terminado con ese verso~~.
He is dead. The poem is done with that verse.

3. **TENER** is used in the expressions:

Tengo hambre/ sed/ frío/ calor/ sueño/miedo/ 40(cuarenta) años,
        prisa, razón, cuidado.
I am hungry/ thirsty/ cold/ hot/ sleepy/scared/40 years old/ in a hurry/
        right/ careful

4. **HACER** is used in expressions related to wheather

Hoy hace calor/ frío/ sol/ viento/ 20 grados/ buen tiempo/ mal tiempo.
Today, it is hot/ cold/ sunny/ windy/ 20 degrees/ good weather/ bad
                                                        weather.

In addition to the differences seen above, some adjectives change their
meaning depending on accompanying "ser" or "estar".

Spanish	English	
	(as "ser")	(as "estar")
aburrido	boring	bored
atento	courteous	attentive
bueno	good	tasty
consciente	aware	conscience
despierto	sharp	awake
interesado	self-seeking	interested
libre	not constrained	unoccupied
listo	smart	ready
nuevo	brand new	new in appearance
rico	rich	tasty
seguro	save	sure
vivo	cunning	alive

Frequently Asked Questions

FAQ 1: Do all infinitives have gender: el cantar (= the singing)?

Yes, they do. This is a hint that they are verbs that became nouns. All infinitives when working as nouns are masculine.

> Me gusta pintar.
> Pintar me gusta.
> **El** pintar me gusta.
> I like painting.

FAQ 2: Do all past participles have gender: cansado/ cansada?

Yes, they do. And this is a hint that they are verbs that become adjectives.

Exercises

Exercise 1

Translate the following sentences into Spanish using the appropriate verb tense: infinitive, gerund, etc.

1. It is important to identify the problem
2. Smoking is bad for your health.
3. To work here you need a special permit.
4. Thank you very much for taking the time to consider me for the position.
5. It took me two hours to realize.
6. Besides working for the fraternity, I practice sports.
7. The decision to set up that opera was a success.
8. With leaving a message you don't not solve anything, you must go in person.
9. Before applying for the job, think about it.
10. After discussing it at the board, we conclude that the product is viable.
11. People working in factories are the ones that suffer the most from that syndrome.
12. When arriving there, get some pictures first.

Answers:

1. Es importante **identificar** bien el problema [error: a identificar*].
2. **Fumar** es malo para la salud [error: fumando].
3. **Para trabajar** aqui necesitas un permiso especial.
4. Muchas gracias por tomarse el tiempo **de considerarme** para la posición [error: para considerarme].
5. Tardé dos horas **en darme** cuenta [error: a darme*].
6. Además **de trabajar** para la fraternidad, hago deporte [error: a trabajar].
7. La decisión **de poner** la ópera fue un acierto [error: poner].
8. **Con dejar** un mensaje no resuelves nada, debes ir en persona [error: con dejando].
9. Antes **de solicitar** el trabajo, piénsalo [error: solitando].
10. Después **de debatirlo** en la mesa directiva, llegamos a la conclusion de que el producto es viable [error: debatiendo].
11. Las personas **que trabajan** en fábricas son las que más sufren de este síndrome [error: trabajando].
12. Cuando **tú llegues** ahí, saca unas fotos primero [error: llegando].

(*) The fragments in the square brackets correspond to common mistakes from English-speaking students.

Exercise 2

Translate the following paragraph using the appropriate past tense: preterite or imperfect.

First rewrite the paragraph in English changing the past tense in those instances where the English past tense is equivalent to: "I used to do," "I was doing," or "when I did..."

When I was young, I sang very well. I took classes at the college from 1980 to 1986. I sang three times abroad. I sang opera and operetta pieces. I trained every day. In 1988, I sang in the Opera of Madrid. But that day, when I sang, a lamp fell on my head and gave me an electric shock. Since then I haven't sung professionally any longer. It was then that I decided to go instrumental music. Two years ago I got my diploma in music, and I have been for two years working on this since then. There was a time that singing was my passion, but that passion, although did not die because no one killed it, gave rise to another more intense and lasting.

Answers:

When I was young, I **used to sing** very well. I took classes at the college from 1980 to 1986. I sang three times abroad. I **used to sing** opera and zarzuela pieces. I **used to train** every day. In 1988, I sang in the Opera of Madrid. But that day, when I **was singing**, a lamp fell on my head and gave me an electric shock. Since then I haven't sung professionally any longer. It was then that I decided to go instrumental music. Two years ago I got my diploma in music, and I have been working on this for two years since then. There was a time that singing was my passion (**There used to be** a time that singing was my passion*), but that passion, although did not die because no one killed it, gave rise to another more intense and lasting.

Cuando yo **era** joven yo **cantaba** muy bien. Tomé clases en el colegio de 1980 a 1986. Canté tres veces en el extranjero. **Cantaba** fragmentos de opera y zarzuelas. **Entrenaba** todos los días. En 1988 canté en el Palacio de la Opera de Madrid. Pero ese día cuando **cantaba**, una lámpara cayó sobre mi cabeza y me dio un golpe eléctrico. Desde entonces no he cantado más profesionalmente. Fue entonces cuando decidí dedicarme a la música instrumental. Hace dos años obtuve mi diploma en música y llevo dos años trabajando en esto desde entonces. Hubo un tiempo que cantar fue mi pasión (**Había** un tiempo que cantar era mi pasión*), pero esa pasión, aunque no murió porque nadie la mató, dio origen a otra más intensa y duradera.

(*) Note that this sentence is correct either way: with preterite or imperfect, since the writer can opt to show that those eight years (when singing was her passion) either as a period of time or just a point in time.

Exercise 3

Translate the following paragraph using the appropriate verb: *ser* or *estar*:

1. Pedro **looks** fat.
2. Pedro **was born** in Colombia.
3. Luisa **lives** in Barcelona.
4. Gracia **is** a well-prepared manager.
5. Gracia **is** well-prepared for that meeting.
6. Moving to another premises **is** decided.
7. I **am** not familiar with that kind of music.
8. Juan **is** bored but he **is** not boring.
9. **Are** you interested in this software application?
10. Lucas only does it to win a promotion. He**'s** very self-seeking.
11. The patient **was** aware of the seriousness of his injuries.
12. The patient **was** awake during the operation.

Answers:

1. Pedro está gordo.
2. Pedro es de Colombia.
3. Luisa está en Barcelona.
4. Gracia es una directora bien preparada.
5. Gracia está bien preparada para esa reunión.
6. Mudarse a otras instalaciones está decidido.
7. No estoy familiarizado con ese tipo de música.
8. Juan está aburrido, pero no es aburrido.
9. ¿Estás interesado en esta aplicación de software?
10. Lucas solo lo hace para ganar un ascenso. Es una persona muy interesada.
11. El paciente era consciente de la gravedad de sus heridas.
12. El paciente no estuvo consciente durante la operación.

8. HOW TO LEARN WORDS EFFICIENTLY
CÓMO APRENDER PALABRAS EFICIENTEMENTE

When you look up certain words in the dictionary, you must look for the proxy of the word.

> e.g. "carro" (singular), not "carros" (plural)
> e.g. "gato" (masculine), not "gata" (feminine)
> e.g. "estudiar" (infinitive), not "estudié" (past tense).

The proxy must be singular and masculine (if the word is a noun, determiner or adjective) and infinitive (if the word is a verb).

As for the meaning, we can classify words in two main categories:

> **Non-grammatical words** are those words with an actual meaning by itself: dog, white, walking, Peter, fast, attitude,…

> **Grammatical words** are those words that create the structure of the sentence: the, a, at, to, over, however, maybe, on, another, by...

You could only communicate very primitively without grammatical words. Grammatical words form the structure of the sentence. For example, in the sentence "Your cat is on the table," if you removed the grammatical words the result would be absurd:

> (Your) cat is (on the) table → cat is table

We recommend the following method. Consider it as a **golden rule.**

> - **Keep records**, specially if you are learning a consistent number of words a week. Flash cards are a great idea to test yourself. Using a computer spreadsheet for those words is the best way to keep a record. It enables you to sort your learned words and keep them organized.
>
> - **Pick your own words**. Make sure you know the grammatical words (*Appendix D List of Grammatical Words*), and pick non-grammatical words from your areas of interest. Families of words work better than unlinked words.
>
> - **Notice if the words you are picking have similarities with English in any form**. Being aware of the commonalities will help you not only memorize the word but also memorize other words of its family.

A distinction can be made regarding the similar words in both languages. On one hand, there are "**cognates**," those words from Spanish that are easy to translate and recognize, for instance teléfono/telephone or artista/artist. On the other hand, there is what we can call "indirect cognates," those words whose similarities are not evident, but are based on other words of the same family. For instance, "agua" is not a cognate of "water;" however, you can find the meaning through the cognate: aquarium/acuario.

There are hundreds of cognates, and hundreds of indirect cognates. Below you will find a list of indirect and direct cognates:

Spanish	English	Cognate English/ Spanish
agua	water	aquarium = acuario
año	year	annual = anual
araña	spider	arachnid = arácnido
árbol	tree	arboretum = arboreto
avión	plane	aviation = aviación
bailar	to dance	ballerina = bailarina
beber	to drink	beverage = bebida
campo	field	to camp = acampar
carne	meat	carnivore = carnívoro
cerebro	brain	cerebral = cerebral
cien	hundred	cent = céntimo

Spanish	English	Cognate English/ Spanish
cuerpo	body	corporal = corporal
diente	tooth	dentist = dentista
dormir	to sleep	dormant = durmiente
escalera	ladder	escalator = escalera mecánica
gemelo	twin	Gemini (zodiac) = géminis
grande	big	grand = gran
hombre	man	human = humano
leche	milk	lactose = lactosa
lengua	tongue	language = lenguaje
luna	moon	lunar = lunar
mano	hand	manual = manual
mar	sea	submarine = submarino
mes	month	semester = semestre
mil	thousand	mile = milla
muerto	dead	morgue = morgue
nacer	to be born	native = nativo
nave	vessel	navigate = navegar
pez	fish	Pisces (zodiac) = piscis
piel	skin	to peel = pelar
polvo	dust	to pulverize = pulverizar
pueblo	village	popular = popular
refugio	shelter	to refuge = refugiar
sentir	to feel	sentiment = sentimiento
sol	sun	solar = solar
toro	bull	Taurus (zodiac) = tauro
uno	one	unit = unidad
vender	to sell	vendor = vendedor
ver	to see	visible = visible
vivir	to live	to survive = sobrevivir

Prefixes and Suffixes

A prefix is an initial part of a word with meaning. It is called suffix if it goes at the end of the word. For example the prefix "un" means "opposite." Thus, for example: "unnecessary" means "not necessary."

The vast majority of prefixes and suffixes are the same or very similar in both Spanish and English. Below, you will find just a sample:

Spanish		English	
in-	e.g. innecesario	un-	e.g. unnecessary
pre-	e.g. prenatal	pre-	e.g. prenatal
post-	e.g. post operación	post-	e.g. post operation
ex-	e.g. exconvicto	ex-	e.g. ex convict
anti-	e.g. antidroga	anti-	e.g. anti drugs
-dad	e.g. integridad	-ty	e.g. integrity
-ción	e.g. preparación	-tion	e.g. preparation
-ismo	e.g. comunismo	-ism	e.g. communism

Both prefixes and suffixes are welded to the main term. The prefix are hyphenated just when the main word is capitalized. The prefix is hyphenated when the main term is capitalized. The prefix is a separate word when the main term is a multiple word.

> ex husband, super boring, pro Obama, ex prime minister
> exmarido, superaburrido, pro-Obama, ex primer ministro

Spanglish

Spanglish is what results when you insert an English word (genuine or altered) in a Spanish speech.

> Si tomo la **freeway**, llego allí antes.

This means: "If I take the freeway, I get there sooner;" where "freeway" is not a Spanish word.

In some cases the word has been taken from English as is (in spelling and pronunciation):

> (la) freeway, (el) bypass,(el) SUV, (el) bill, (los) taxes,
> (el) VCR, (el) U-turn, (el) e-mail, (el) zip code

Other times, the words have suffered some adaptation to the Spanish pronunciation:

> la troca (= truck), la marketa (= market), la carpeta (= carpet), la yarda (= yard), las utilidades (= utilities), las partes (= auto-parts), lonchear (= to have lunch), parkear (= to park), likear (= to leak)

Occasionally, the newborn word can conflict with another word existing in the Spanish standard:

Non-standard Spanish	Standard Spanish
carpeta (= carpet)	carpeta (= folder)
remover (= to remove)	remover (= to stir)
ordenar (= to order food)	ordenar (= to command)

Those words that sound similar in both languages but have different meanings are called false cognates or "false friends." You can't trust them: their meaning is different to what you would expect.

In Spanish	sounds like...	but it means...
embarazada	embarrassing	pregnant
recuerdo	record	a memory
consistente	consistent	firm, fix

This section is just to warn you that those words exist and that they are part of the common speech in the U.S. However, those words are not in the dictionary, and, they may not be understood by the speakers of the Spanish-speaking countries.

Frequently Asked Questions

FAQ 1: Where do I find the "grammatical words"?

You probably know all of them. You need them when you communicate in Spanish. You can test yourself by using the list in *Appendix D List of Grammatical Words.*

About which non-grammatical words to learn, this is a personal choice. For example, one can enjoy learning words related with cars, cooking, business, etc.

The effort of finding the words you like is half of the learning process: you memorize when you search.

Even when you can communicate and speak a language with precision, you always have words to learn and to enjoy learning.

FAQ 2: "Piecito" o "piececito, for "small foot"?

Spanish has a full range of diminutives suffixes (suffixes meaning "small"): ito, ecito, ececito, illo, ecillo, ico, ino, uelo.

In the case of ito, cita, cecito, to form the diminutive, you can add the suffix "ito" to the base, or "ecito," "ececito" if the word ends with "e." The use or "ecito" vs. "ececito" is just a dialectal preference. "Piececito" is preferred in Spain, and "piecito" in latin America.

```
casa:     cas   + ita       → casita (= small house)
clase:    clase + ecita     → clasecita (= small classroom)
pie:      pie   + ecito     → piecito (= small foot)
pie:      pie   + ececito   → piececito (= small foot)
```


FAQ 3: "Calentito" o "calientito, for "a bit hot"?

Calentito. The reason why we say "caliente" and not ~~calente~~ has to do with the point of stress. In Spanish the **stressed** "e" tends to transform into a "ie:" For example, we say hielo (= ice), but we don't say ~~hielado~~ but "helado" (= iced) because the "e" is not stressed

The original adjective is "caliente" and it is the stressed "e" what justifies the transformation to "ie," but in "calentito" the stress is not on the "e," so its derivatives, as calentito or calenturiento (= randy), don't change the "e."

Exercises

Find in the dictionary related words of the words and expressions below, and translate them. They can be content or root related:

#	Spanish	English	Answer
1.	al final	At the end of the day	Por fin (= at last), por último, finalmente (= finally), ultimatum (=ultimatum)
2.	muela	molar	moler (= to grind), demoler (= to demolish)
3.	adjetivo	adjective	ad- (= joined), adverbio (= adverb), adicionar (= to add), admitir (= to admit)
4.	a sangre fría	at sang froid, in cold blood	sanguinario (= sanguinary), consanguineo (= consanguineous), sangría (= sangria drink)
5.	mantener	to maintain	tener (= to have got), contener (= to contain), detener (= to detain)
6.	criticar	to critique	situación crítica (= critical situation), una critica (= criticism), la critica literaria (= literary critique)
7.	educar	to educate	educado * (= well-behaved), culto (= well-educated)
8.	individuo	individual	Un caso individual (= an individual case)
9.	nacional	national	vuelo nacional (= domestic flight), nacer (= to be born), Navidad (= Nativity, Christmas)
10.	manzano	apple tree	naranjo (= orange tree), cerezo (=cherry tree), limonero (= lemon tree)

(*) Some terms can be "false friends" (similar in both language but with different meaning). This kind of exercise also help catch these words.

APPENDICES

APPENDIX A

NOTES ABOUT DIALECTS
NOTAS SOBRE DIALECTOS

APPENDIX A: NOTES ABOUT DIALECTS
NOTAS SOBRE DIALECTOS

All languages have dialects. In the same way that English speakers from United Kingdom, Ireland, United States or Australia speak the same language differently; speakers from Spain, Argentina or Mexico have recognizable differences.

Nonetheless, Spanish is a very unified language. The rules of grammar and spelling are the same all over the Spanish-speaking world. The differences between dialects are limited mostly to the preference of some words over others, and some differences in the pronunciation.

English	Example 1	Example 2
US English	line	tomato /tomeito/
UK English	queue	tomato /tomatoh/

Spanish		
Mexican Spanish	fila (= line)	jitomate (= tomato)
Spanish from Spain	cola	tomate

The Spanish spoken in the southwest of United States (mostly California, Arizona, Texas and New Mexico) belongs to the realm of the Mexican dialect. In addition, Spanish in the US is, of course, influenced by the English language, and some words used in the US are not part of the standard.

	Example 1	Example 2	Example 3
English	market	carpet	truck
US Spanish	marketa*	carpeta*	troca*
Spanish	mercado	alfombra	camión

(*) Not standard Spanish

A language can be divided into dialects and, in turn, those dialects can be subdivided into subdialects indefinitely. However, we can consider three main dialects with the following representatives:

- Spanish from Spain
- Spanish from Latin America (except Argentina)
- Spanish from Argentina

The most apparent difference among the dialects in Spanish is the use of the pronouns and the verb forms thereof, as shown in the following table:

	Spain	Latin America	Argentina
I sing	(yo) canto	← THE SAME	← THE SAME
You (singular) sing	(tú) cantas	← THE SAME	(vos) cantás *
He/She sings	(él /ella) canta	← THE SAME	← THE SAME
We sing	(nosotros) cantamos	← THE SAME	← THE SAME
You guys sing	(vosotros) cantáis	(ustedes) cantan	← THE SAME
They sing	(ellos) cantan	← THE SAME	← THE SAME

(*) Notice that the stress is on the last "a."

When addressing someone **formally**, the pronouns used are the same in all three dialects:

	Spain	Latin America	Argentina
sir/ ma'am, you sing	(usted) canta	← THE SAME	← THE SAME
sirs/ ma'ams, you sing	(ustedes) cantan	← THE SAME	← THE SAME

Thus, only in Spain there is a distinction for the form "you:" vosotros (informal), ustedes (formal).

Spanish from Spain

Except in its Southern area, Spain uses the English *th* **sound** for both the letter **z**, and the letter **c** when combined in **ce**, **ci** (as is taught in this book).

In Spain, they use **vosotros** (= you guys). Vosotros is one form taught in this book. In Spain, they also use "usted" (= you singular) and "ustedes" (= you plural), but only either to mark a distance from the person you are addressing, like addressing a stranger, or to show respect, like addressing a professor.

Usted uses the forms of "él/ella," e.g. "Usted estudia mucho." In the same way, "ustedes" uses the forms of "ellos," e.g. "Ustedes estudian mucho."

Only in Spain, the second person of plural and its pronouns are used, which are:

> **"vosotros"** (or vosotras) as in **"vosotros cantáis"** (– you guys study). In Latin America: "**ustedes cantan.**"

> **"vuestro"** (or "vuestra," "vuestros," "vuestras") as in "vuestro amigo" (= the friend of you guys). In Latin America: "**Su** amigo."

> "**os**" as in "Os canto" (= I sing to you guys). In Latin America: "**Les** canto."

A rule to use the forms of **vosotros** is simply to substitute the ending "mos" of **nosotros** for "is." Thus,

> Nosotros canta**mos** → Vosotros cant**áis**
> Nosotros bebe**mos** → Vosotros beb**éis**
> Nosotros viví**mos** → Vosotros viv**ís**

> (= We sing, drink, live -- You guys sing, drink, live)

This rule works for most of the irregular verbs too, e.g. dormir (= to sleep)

> Nosotros dormi**mos** → Vosotros dorm**ís**

There are three exceptions:

a) The verb "haber" (= to have)

> Nosotros he**mos** estudiado → Vosotros hab**éis** estudiado
> (no: Vosotros ~~heis~~ estudiado)

> (= We have studied -- You guys have studied)

b) The nosotros form when ending in "imos". In this case, the vosotros form will have only one "i," e.g. :

> Nosotros vivi**mos** → Vosotros viv**ís**
> (not: Vosotros ~~viviis~~)
> (= We live -- You guys live)

c) The past tense. For this tense, the vosotros form can be created out
of the "tú" form just by adding "is," e.g.:

> Tú cantaste → Vosotros cantaste**is**
> Tú bebiste → Vosotros bebiste**is**
> Tú vivíste → Vosotros viviste**is**

Spanish from Latin America

In Latin America, **they use the /s/ sound for the letter c when
combined in ce, ci, and the letter z** (instead of the /th/ sound used in
Spain). So, they don't distinguish between caza (= hunting) and casa
(= house), or between coser (= to sew) and cocer (= to boil.)

Latin America **never uses "vosotros."** Instead, "ustedes" is used.
Remember: "ustedes" uses the forms of "ellos" e.g. "Ustedes estudian
mucho."

In some areas of Latin America, they never use "tú." They use
"usted" instead. Remember: "usted" uses the forms of "él/ella" e.g.
"Usted estudia mucho."

Spanish from Argentina

In regards to the characteristics of the Spanish spoken in Latin
America, Argentina shows two specific differences: the use of **"vos,"**
and the pronunciation of the **strong "ll."**

Argentina has a very strong pronunciation of both the "ll," and the
"y" as a consonant. It sounds close to the English "g" in George or
the "sh" in shoe, depending on the speaker.

Argentina uses "vos" (= you singular) instead of "tú." Generally
speaking, "vos" goes with the forms of "vosotros" but eliminates the -
i- of the last syllable. Example:

> vosotros cantáis → vos cantás.

This rule only applies for the simple present (vos cantás).

The Imperative (the commands) also makes a transformation from the original "vosotros." It uses the form of vosotros but eliminates the final "d."

Cantad vosotros → cantá vos

The rest of the tenses follow the standard rules of conjugation.

"Vos" does not have its own set of associated pronouns, so it uses the ones of "tú." Examples:

Vos, a **tu** manera… (= you, in your way, …).
A vos **te** canta María (= Maria sings to you).
No tenés que ir**te** (= You don't have to go).

The use of vos is called "voseo." Argentina is where voseo is norm. Uruguay and Paraguay and areas of Central America use "vos," but their rules are not consistent, and it is not considered standard Spanish.

APPENDIX B

WORDS OF SPAIN AND LATIN AMERICA
PALABRAS DE ESPAÑA Y LATINOAMÉRICA

APPENDIX B: WORDS OF SPAIN AND LATIN AMERICA
PALABRAS DE ESPAÑA Y LATINOAMÉRICA

You may have heard the term **"castellano"** (*castellano* literally means "from Castile," the central region in Spain). In Spanish, this word has two meanings. One is another word for "Spanish language." Thus, a person from Peru, Mexico, or Buenos Aires can claim: "Hablo castellano" (= I speak Spanish). The other meaning is the dialect of Spanish spoken in the region of Castile, in the central and northern Spain. Thus, you, as a student can say: "Hablo -el dialecto- castellano" (= I speak the Castilian dialect). "Castellano" is the adjective of "Castilla" (= Castile). Castile was one the kingdoms that formed Spain and also where the Spanish language was originated.

The terms "Spanish from Spain" and "Castilian dialect" are the same. However, two areas of Spain: Southern Spain and the Canary Islands (both outside the the region of Castile) deviate some from the Castilian dialect. In southern Spain, they don't use the lisp (the English "th" pronunciation). In the Canary Islands, in addition to the lack of the lisp, they don't use the "vosotros" form. (Consequently, according to Appendix A, the Canary Islands fits into the Latin American dialect!).

In addition to this, **in Spain there are three other languages**: Catalan, Galician and Basque, which are spoken in six Autonomous Communities. In these **bilingual** communities, the Spanish dialect in use is the Castilian dialect.

Recapitulating *Appendix A, Notes about Dialects*, the main identifiers of the Castilian dialect are: the use of the "vosotros" forms, and the "lisp" (the English "th" pronuntiation). **Other differences are:**

- The use of both endings "-se" and "-ra," with no preference, for the forms of the Past Subjunctive. In Latin America the form "ra" is preferred.

Habría pintado la casa si hubiera [or: hubiese] tenido tiempo (in Spain).
Habría pintado la casa si hubiera tenido tiempo (in Latin America).
I would have painted my hose if I had had time

- The use of the Present Perfect (He cantado = I have sung). Outside Castile, it is common to use the Preterite (Canté = I sang) instead.

Gracias, he comido muy bien (in Spain).
Gracias, comí muy bien (in Latin America).
Thank you, I have eaten very well.

- The use of "le" as a direct object pronoun, just for persons, masculine and singular. This variation is accepted (See *Chapter 4 Pronouns*, FAQ 3).

Juan está bien. Le vi ayer (in Spain).
Juan está bien. Lo vi ayer (in Latin America).
Juan is fine. I saw him yesterday.

The following is a **list of words used in Spain** that are uncommon in Latin America. Be aware that the terms displayed in this list are a generalization, and there may be areas in Latin America that use the same terms as in Spain.

English	In Spain		In Latin America	
accountant	el	contable		contador
angry		enfadado		enojado, bravo, moles
apartment, flat	el	piso	el	apartamento
band-aid	la	tirita	la	curita
bean	la	judía	el	frijol
beautiful		bonito		lindo
bedroom	el	dormitorio	la	recámara
blazer	la	americana	el	saco
blonde		rubio		güero
bowl	el	cuenco	la	jícara
bribe	el	soborno	la	mordida
car (automobile)	el	coche	el	carro
carpet	la	moqueta	el	alfombrado
cell phone	el	móvil	el	celular
chauffeur	el	chofér	el	chofer
check book	el	talonario	la	chequera

English	In Spain		In Latin America	
cigarette	el	cigarrillo	el	cigarro
computer	el	ordenador	el/la	computador/ora
concrete	el	hormigón	el	concreto
court	el	tribunal	la	corte
directions	las	señas	la	dirección
elevator, lift	el	ascensor	el	elevador
father	el	padre	el	papá
first payment	el	depósito, entrada	el	enganche
gang	la	banda	la	panda
gas station	la	gasolinera	la	bomba
tomato (red)	el	tomate	la	jitomate
hair	el	pelo	el	cabello
herb store	el	herbolario	la	botánica
insurance	el	seguro	la	aseguranza
juice	el	zumo	el	jugo
kid	el	niño	el	escuincle
lawn	el	césped	el	zacate, la grama
light bulb	la	bombilla	el	foco
match	la	cerilla	el	fósforo
meeting	la	reunión	la	junta
mother	la	madre	la	mamá
not any more		ya no		nomás
OK		vale		okey
pastry	el	bollo	el	pan dulce
pajamas	el	pijama	los	piyamas
to park		aparcar		estacionar
peach	el	melocotón	el	durazno
peanut	el	cacahuete	el	cacahuate, maní
pig	el	cerdo	el	puerco
piggy bank	la	hucha	la	alcancia
please		por favor		favor
possum	la	zarigüeya	el	tlacuache, rabipelado
potato	la	patata	la	papa
radio	la	radio	el	radio
real estate	los	inmuebles	los	bienes raíces
rope	la	cuerda	la	soga
shrimp	la	gamba	el	camarón
skunk	la	mofeta	el	zorrillo
speaker (person)	el	portavoz	el	vocero
stamp	el	sello	la	estampilla
student	el	alumno	el	estudiante

English		In Spain		In Latin America
sweater	el	jersey, suéter	el	suéter, pulóver
swimming pool	la	piscina	la	alberca, la pileta
to check		comprobar		chequear
to come back		volver		regresar
to delay		tardar		demorar
to drink (alcohol)		beber (alcoh.)		tomar
to drive		conducir		manejar
to get in a hurry		apresurarse		apurarse
to get nervous		poner nervioso		dar ansia
to grab		coger		agarrar
to have a chance		tener oportunidad		tener chance
to jump		saltar		brincar
to miss someone		echar de menos		extrañar
to monitor		monitorizar		monitorear
to park		aparcar		estacionar
to pull		tirar		jalar
to stand		estar de pie		estar parado
to stand up		levantarse		pararse
to turn on		encender		prender
to talk		hablar		platicar
to tie		atar		amarrar
to toss		echar		botar
unemployed	el	parado	el	desempleado
univ. dormitory	el	colegio mayor	la	residencia estudiantil
useful contact	el	enchufe	la	palanca
VCR	el	vídeo	el	video

For additional reference, the following is a list of terms commonly used in Spain related to **education and the day-to-day live**.

Spanish		English
la	asociación de estudiantes	sorority or fraternity
la	autoescuela	driving school
la	beca	scholarship
el	bocadillo	a sandwich generally of a loaf bread
el	bote	the tips' jar (propina = tip)
el	café con leche	café au lait
el	café cortado	machiatto (espresso with milk)
el	café solo	expresso

Spanish		English
la	caña	a glass of beer of approx. 8 Oz.
el	catedrático	chair of the department (college)
la	clase	class, classroom, course
el	colegio	elementary and middle school center
el	colegio mayor	dormitory (univ.)
el	Colegio oficial de abogados, ingeneros, etc.	Board of attorneys, engineers, etc.
el/la	director/a	principal of a school
la	escuela de ingenieros	engineering college
la	ESO, Educación Secundaria Obligatoria	High School Education
la	facultad	college (excluding engineering studies)
la	guardería	day care
el	instituto	High School Center
el	menú del día	menu of the day, dish of the day
la	primaria	elementary and middle school educ.
el	PVP, Precio de Venta al Público	final price, including taxes
la	ración	dish of food
la	rectoría	dean's office (univ.)
la	tapa	a small portion of food, free
la	universidad	university, college
el	telediario	TV news

APPENDIX C

NOTES ABOUT CULTURE
NOTAS SOBRE CULTURA

APPENDIX C: NOTES ABOUT CULTURE
NOTAS SOBRE CULTURA

In the process of communicating with a patient some knowledge about the culture of the speaker can be crucial. Below are some features that may be distinctive of the culture in the Spanish speaking countries.

1. Figures

Remember that the Spanish word **billón** doesn't mean *billion*. Instead, one **billón** equals 1000 billions.

> 1,000,000,000 es mil millones.
> 1,000,000,000 is one billion.
>
> 1,000,000,000,000 es un billón.
> 1,000,000,000,000 is one thousand billion.

Spanish never expresses figures neither in tens nor in hundreds.

> 1900 es mil novecientos.
> 1900 is nineteen hundred.
>
> 1995 es mil novecientos noventa y cinco
> 1995 is nineteen, ninety five.

Unlike English, in Spanish the comma is frequently used to indicate decimal and the period is used to indicate thousands.

> Pi es 3,14 aproximadamente.
> Pi is 3.14 approximately.

2.000 es dos mil.
2,000 is two thousand.

In Spanish, monetary figures have the symbol of the currency at the end.

2.000,50 $ son dos mil dólares y cincuenta centavos.
$2,000.50 is two thousand dollars and fifty cents.

2. Units of Measurement

Many countries only use units of measurement of the International Systems
(also called metric system, or decimal system).

Below is a table with the names of the units, their abbreviations, and their
conversion to U.S. system units.

Abrev.	Spanish	English	Conversion
g	gramo	gram	1 g = 0.03 oz (onzas de peso)
Kg	kilo	kilo	1 Kg = Lb (libras)
m	metro	meter	1 m =3.28 ft (pies)
cm	centímetro	centimeter	1 cm =0.39 inch (pulgadas)
Km	kilómetro	kilometer	1 Km = 0.62 miles (millas)
l	litro	liter	1 l = 0.26 gal (galones) 1 l = 33.81 fl oz (onzas de líquido)
°C	Celsius	Celsius	37 C = 98.6 °F (Fahrenheit) * 38 C = 100.4 °F 39 C = 102.2 °F

(*) The conversion from Celsius to Fahrenheit is not linear. The
formulae is: $°F = (°C \times 9/5) + 32$

3. Dates

Dates are given in this order: day, month, and year:

31/01/12 es el treinta y uno de enero de dos mil doce.
01/31/12 is January thirty first, two thousand twelve.

Years, as any figure, are **never** expressed in tens or hundreds. (See "Figures"
above).

In Spanish calendars, the week starts on Monday (not on Sunday).

4. Tú vs. Usted

In those regions where both **tú** and **usted** are used (some regions only use usted), "tú" is used to address someone informally, and "usted," formally.

Every Spanish-speaking country has its different social codes, and they accept "tú" in different levels of familiarity. This is why it is recommended that you use "usted" always, unless the person addresses you differently.

Usted is commonly abbreviated as Ud. or Vd.; and **ustedes,** as Uds. or Vds.

5. Courtesy

Use **por favor** (= please) extensively. It could sound rude otherwise, specially with commands.

> Por favor, puedes venir por aquí (not: Ven por aquí).
> Please, can you come this way.

Smiling and using the courtesy tags will really help you gain a person's confidence and respect.

> Gracias. De nada. Por favor. Lo siento.
> Thank you. You're welcome. Please. I am sorry.

6. The Two Last Names

In many Spanish speaking countries the naming system includes the father's and mother's paternal family names.

The first name, **el nombre** or **el nombre de pila** (= the Baptism name) can be one or more names, i.e. José Carlos, Marco Antonio.

The first surname, **el apellido**, or **el primer apellido**, or **el apellido del padre** (= the father's surname) is always the person's father's last name.

The second surname, **el segundo apellido**, or **el apellido de la madre** (= the mother's surname) is the person mother's last name.

For example, Antonio Álvarez Ala and Beatriz Barroso Barrio's have a child. They name him Luis. Consequently, Luis' full name is: Luis Álvarez Barroso.

7. The Pace of the Day

The stages of the day are: **la mañana**, which lasts from the sunrise until lunch time (at 1, 2 or even 3 pm); **la tarde**, until sunset; and **la noche**, when it's dark. So, Spanish doesn't distinguish between afternoon and evening. They both are **la tarde**.

The strongest meal of the day is commonly **la comida** or **el almuerzo** (= lunch). **El desayuno** and **la cena** (=breakfast and dinner) are lighter meals. All these meals are typically taken later than their counterparts in the English culture. In addition, people may have a snack before lunch, called **el aperitivo**, or before dinner, called **la merienda**.

Traditionally, people have a nap, **la siesta**, after lunch. It is believed that this tradition is a result of having a heavy meal and high temperatures at the time of that meal. One common characteristic of the Spanish-speaking countries is the hot climate. Spain enjoys hot summers; so does her sister countries in the Americas. Even Argentina and Chile, with extreme latitude, have regions with hot summers. Nowadays, work schedules with long commutes and short lunch breaks don't allow time for this nap; however, in summertime and during holidays more people have a nap after lunch in those countries.

8. Greetings

It is extended in the Spanish-speaking world to give one **beso** (= kiss) or two on the cheeks as a way of greeting. The kiss exchange occurs woman-woman or man-woman, and it is used among family and friends.

APPENDIX D

LIST OF GRAMMATICAL WORDS
LISTA DE PALABRAS GRAMATICALES

APPENDIX D: LIST OF GRAMMATICAL WORDS
LISTA DE PALABRAS GRAMATICALES

The following is a list of words with grammatical meaning as explained in the text.

In the following table:

- Underscore indicates the point of stress. One vowel words or words with accent mark are not indicated.

- The ellipses (…) at the end of a term indicates that the word must be followed by a noun or an adjective, i.e. "any…" in "any person can do it" vs "any" in "any can do it." The ellipses between two words indicates there is some content in between, e.g. "either or".

- A capitalized initial indicates the word or expression can function as a complete sentence, e.g. Hello.

- Notice that no indication about the gender (masculine/ feminine) is needed: none of these words are nouns (nouns are not grammatical words)

#	English	Spanish
1	a	un , una
2	a lot	mucho
3	a lot of...	mucho/a/os/as
4	according to	según
5	after	tras
6	against	contra
7	all	todo/a/os/as el/la/los/las...
8	although	aunque
9	and	y
10	another	otro/ a
11	any, whichever	cualquiera
12	any..., whichever	cualquier...
13	around...	alrededor de...
14	as	a medida que
15	as	como
16	as per	en cuanto a...
17	as soon as	tan pronto como
18	at	en, a
19	at/ in the beginning of...	al principio de...
20	at/ in the end of...	al final de
21	because	porque
22	because of	por
23	because of	por causa de
24	between, among	entre
25	both	los dos
26	but	pero
27	but	sino
28	by	por
29	due to	debido a
30	either...or...	o...o..
31	everything	todo
32	excuse me	Con permiso
33	far from	lejos de
34	for	para, por
35	from	desde, de
36	given that	dado que

#	English	Spanish
37	Good afternoon	Buenas tardes
38	Good evening, night	Buenas noches
39	Good morning	Buenos días
40	Goodbye	Adiós
41	he	él
42	Hello	Hola
43	Help me!	¡Ayuda!
44	Help me!	¡Socorro!
45	her	su / sus
46	here	aquí, acá
47	hers	suyo /a / os / as
48	his (as in "his house")	su / sus
49	his (as in "This is his")	suyo /a / os / as
50	how (quest. & exclam.)	cómo
51	How long ago…?	¿Cuánto tiempo hace…?
52	How long…?	¿Por cuánto tiempo…?
53	How many…?	¿Cuánto/a/os/as…?
54	How much…?	¿Cuánto/a...?
55	How often…?	¿Con qué frecuencia…?
56	However	sin embargo
57	I	yo
58	I don't know.	No lo sé, No sé.
59	I wish!	Ojalá
60	I'm sorry	Perdón, Lo siento.
61	if	si
62	in	en
63	in case that	en el caso de que
64	in other words	en otras palabras
65	in spite of	a pesar de
66	in the middle of…	en medio de…
67	in view that	en vista de que, visto que
68	inside…	dentro de...
69	it	ello (to be omitted)
70	Its	su/ sus
71	Its	suyo /a / os / as
72	like	al igual que

#	English	Spanish
73	like	como
74	little (amount)	poco
75	little (amount)...	poco/a ...
76	Maybe	Tal vez, Quizá(s)
77	Me neither	Yo tampoco
78	Me too	Yo también
79	me, as in "for me"	mí
80	mine	mío/ a/ os/ as
81	much	mucho / mucha
82	much	muchos/as
83	my	mi / mis
84	near, close to, around...	cerca de...
85	neither ...nor...	ni...ni...
86	never	nunca , jamás
87	nevertheless	no obstante
88	next to...	junto a...
89	no	no
90	no...	ningún /ninguna
91	nine	ninguno / ninguna
92	none of...	ninguno/a de ...
93	not	no
94	nothing	nada
95	now	ahora
96	of the	del = de el
97	of you guys	su, vuestro/a/os/as (Sp.)
98	of, from, off	de
99	Okay	Okey
100	on	sobre, en
101	on top of...	encima de...
102	or	o
103	other, others	otro/ a/ os /as
104	our, ours	nuestro/ a / os/ as
105	outside...	fuera de...
106	Please	Por favor
107	Really?	¿De verdad?
108	Right?	¿Verdad?

#	English	Spanish
109	See you later	Hasta la vista
110	See you later	Hasta luego
111	See you soon	Hasta pronto
112	she	ella
113	side by side…	al lado de
114	since	puesto que, ya que
115	so that	para que
116	some	alguno /alguna
117	some of …	alguno/a/os/as de…
118	some…	algún /a /os/ as, unos, unas
119	something	algo
120	supposing that	suponiendo que
121	Thank you	Gracias
122	Thank you very much	Muchas Gracias
123	that	aquel, aquella,aquello
124	that	ese/a, eso
125	the	el, la, los, las
126	their	su / sus
127	theirs	suyo /a / os / as
128	then, afterwards	entonces, luego
129	there	ahí, allí, allá
130	these	estos/as
131	they	ellos
132	this	este/a, esto
133	those	esos/as
134	those (farther)	aquellos/as
135	to	para, a
136	to herself	le, la, se
137	to herself	se
138	to him	le, lo, se
139	to himself	se
140	to it	le, la, lo, se
141	to itself	se
142	to me, to myself	me
143	to the, at the	al = a el
144	to themselves	se

#	English	Spanish
145	to us, to ourselves	nos
146	to you (plural)	les, se
147	to you (s.), to yourself	te
148	to you guys, yourselves	os (Spain)
149	to, at	a
150	to, towards	hacia
151	today	hoy
152	tomorrow	mañana
153	under...	bajo...
154	underneath	debajo de / abajo de
155	unless	a menos que
156	until, up to	hasta
157	we	nosotros
158	what (in other cases)	que
159	what (quest. & exclam.)	qué
160	when	cuando, cuándo
161	where	donde, dónde
162	which (in other cases)	cual/cuales, cuál/cuáles
164	while, as long as	mientras
165	who	quien/quienes, quién/quiénes
166	with	con
167	with me	conmigo
168	with you (s.) informal	contigo
169	without	sin
171	yes	sí
172	yesterday	ayer
173	you (s.), as in "for you"	ti
174	you (singular)	tú
175	you guys	ustedes
176	you guys	vosotros (Spain)
177	You're welcome	De nada
178	your	su / sus (informal)
179	your	tu / tus (singular)
180	yours	suyo /a /os /as (de usted)
181	yours	tuyo/ a / os /as (de ti)

APPENDIX E

TABLE OF ENDINGS
OF REGULAR VERBS
TABLA DE TERMINACIONES
DE LOS VERBOS REGULARES

APPENDIX E: TABLE OF ENDINGS OF REGULAR VERBS
TABLA DE TERMINACIONES DE LOS VERBOS REGULARES

Impersonal Forms of the Verb

Infinitive (to sing)

AR verbs	ER verbs	IR verbs
-ar	-er	-ir

Gerund (singing)

AR verbs	ER verbs	IR verbs
-ando	-iendo	-iendo

Past Participle (sung)

AR verbs	ER verbs	IR verbs
-ado	-ido	-ido

Personal Forms of the Verb: Indicative Mood

Present (I sing)

	AR verbs	ER verbs	IR verbs
(I)	-o	-o	-o
(you singular)	-as	-es	-es
(he/she/it)	-a	-e	-e
(we)	-amos	-emos	-imos
(you guys) -Spain-	-ais	-éis	-ís
(you guys/ they)	-an	-en	-en

Preterite (I sang)

	AR verbs	ER verbs	IR verbs
(I)	-é	-í	-í
(you singular)	-aste	-iste	-iste
(he/she/it)	-ó	-ió	-ió
(we)	-amos	-imos	-imos
(you guys) -Spain-	-asteis	-isteis	-isteis
(you guys/ they)	-aron	-ieron	-ieron

Imperfect Past (I sang*)

	AR verbs	ER verbs	IR verbs
(I)	-aba	-ía	-ía
(you singular)	-abas	-ías	-ías
(he/she/it)	-aba	-ía	-ía
(we)	-ábamos	-íamos	-íamos
(you guys) -Spain-	-abais	-íais	-íais
(you guys/ they)	-aban	-ían	-ían

Future (I will sing)

	AR verbs	ER verbs	IR verbs
(I)	-aré	-eré	-iré
(you singular)	-arás	-erás	-irás
(he/she/it)	-ará	-erá	-irá
(we)	-aremos	-eremos	-iremos
(you guys) -Spain-	-aréis	-eréis	-iréis
(you guys/ they)	-arán	-erán	-irán

Conditional (I would sing)

	AR verbs	ER verbs	IR verbs
(I)	-aría	-ería	-iría
(you singular)	-arías	-erías	-irías
(he/she/it)	-aría	-ería	-iría
(we)	-aríamos	-eríamos	-iríamos
(you guys) -Spain-	-aríais	-eríais	-iríais
(you guys/ they)	-arían	-erían	-irían

Personal Forms of the Verb: Imperative Mood

Imperative (Sing!)

	AR verbs	ER verbs	IR verbs
(I)			
(you singular)	-a	-e	-e
(he/she/it)			
(we)			
(you guys) -Spain-	-ad	-ed	-id
(you guys/ they)			

Personal Forms of the Verb: Subjunctive Mood

Present (...that I sing)

	AR verbs	ER verbs	IR verbs
(I)	-e	-a	-a
(you singular)	-es	-as	-as
(he/she/it)	-e	-a	-a
(we)	-emos	-amos	-amos
(you guys) -Spain-	-éis	-áis	-áis
(you guys/ they)	-en	-an	-an

Past (...that I sang)

	AR verbs	ER verbs	IR verbs
(I)	-ara	-iera	-iera
(you singular)	-aras	-ieras	-ieras
(he/she/it)	-ara	-iera	-iera
(we)	-áramos	-iéramos	-iéramos
(you guys) -Spain-	-arais	-ierais	-ierais
(you guys/ they)	-aran	-ieran	-ieran

-or-

	AR verbs	ER verbs	IR verbs
(I)	-ase	-iese	-iese
(you singular)	-ases	-ieses	-ieses
(he/she/it)	-ase	-iese	-iese
(we)	-ásemos	-iésemos	-iésemos
(you guys) -Spain-	-aseis	-ieseis	-ieseis
(you guys/ they)	-asen	-iesen	-iesen

APPENDIX F

TABLE OF AUXILIARY VERBS:
HABER, ESTAR, SER, IR
TABLE DE LOS VERBOS AUXILIARES:
HABER, ESTAR, SER, IR

APPENDIX F: TABLE OF AUXILIARY VERBS:
HABER, ESTAR, SER, IR
TABLE DE LOS VERBOS AUXILIARES:
HABER, ESTAR, SER, IR

Impersonal Forms of the Verb

Infinitive (to sing)

HABER	ESTAR	SER	IR
haber	estar	ser	ir

Gerund (singing)

habiendo	estando	siendo	yendo

Past Participle (sung)

habido	estado	sido	ido

Personal Forms of the Verb: Indicative Mood

Present (I sing)

	HABER	ESTAR	SER	IR
(I)	he	estoy	soy	voy
(you singular)	has	estás	eres	vas
(he/she/it)	ha	está	es	va
(we)	hemos	estamos	somos	vamos
(you guys) -Spain-	habéis	estáis	sois	vais
(you guys/ they)	han	están	son	van

Preterite (I sang)

	HABER	ESTAR	SER	IR
(I)	hube	estuve	fui	fui
(you singular)	hubiste	estuviste	fuiste	fuiste
(he/she/it)	hubo	estuvo	fue	fue
(we)	hubimos	estuvimos	fuimos	fuimos
(you guys) -Spain-	hubisteis	estuvisteis	fuisteis	fuisteis
(you guys/ they)	hubieron	estuvieron	fueron	fueron

Imperfect (I sang*)

	HABER	ESTAR	SER	IR
(I)	había	estaba	era	iba
(you singular)	habías	estabas	eras	ibas
(he/she/it)	había	estaba	era	iba
(we)	habíamos	estábamos	éramos	íbamos
(you guys) -Spain-	habíais	estabais	erais	ibais
(you guys/ they)	habían	estaban	eran	iban

Future (I´ll sing)	HABER	ESTAR	SER	IR
(I)	habré	estaré	seré	iré
(you singular)	habrás	estarás	serás	irás
(he/she/it)	habrás	estará	será	irá
(we)	habremos	estaremos	seremos	iremos
(you guys) -Spain-	habréis	estaréis	seréis	iréis
(you guys/ they)	habrán	estarán	serán	irán

Conditional (I´d sing)	HABER	ESTAR	SER	IR
(I)	habría	estaría	sería	iría
(you singular)	habrías	estarías	serías	irías
(he/she/it)	habría	estaría	sería	iría
(we)	habríamos	estaríamos	seríamos	iríamos
(you guys)	habríais	estaríais	seríais	iríais
(they)	habrían	estarían	serían	irían

Personal Forms of the Verb:Imperative Mood

Imperative (Sing!)	HABER	ESTAR	SER	IR
(I)				
(you singular)		estate	sé	ve
(he/she/it)				
(we)				
(you guys) -Spain-		estad, estaos	sed	id
(you guys/ they)				

Personal Forms of the Verb: Subjunctive Mood

Pres. (...that I sing)	HABER	ESTAR	SER	IR
(I)	haya	esté	sea	vaya
(you singular)	hayas	estés	seas	vayas
(he/she/it)	haya	esté	sea	vaya
(we)	hayamos	estemos	seamos	vayamos
(you guys) -Spain-	hayáis	estéis	seáis	vayáis
(you guys/ they)	hayan	estén	sean	vayan

Past (...that I sang)	HABER	ESTAR	SER	IR
(I)	hubiera	estuviera	fuera	fuera
(you singular)	hubieras	estuvieras	fueras	fueras
(he/she/it)	hubiera	estuviera	fuera	fuera
(we)	hubiéramos	estuviéramos	fuéramos	fuéramos
(you guys) -Spain-	hubierais	estuvierais	fuerais	fuerais
(you guys/ they)	hubieran	estuvieran	fueran	fueran
-or-				
(I)	hubiese	estuviese	fuese	fuese
(you singular)	hubieses	estuvieses	fueses	fueses
(he/she/it)	hubiese	estuviese	fuese	fuese
(we)	hubiésemos	estuviésemos	fuésemos	fuésemos
(you guys) -Spain-	hubieseis	estuvieseis	fueseis	fueseis
(you guys/ they)	hubiesen	estuviesen	fuesen	fuesen

GLOSSARY

GLOSSARY
GLOSARIO

The following is a list of the linguistic terms used in this book. Every entry includes a reference to the chapter which is relevant to the term in question.

accent mark   The symbol (') that indicates where the stress is

acronym   An abbreviation that actually forms a word. For example: NATO, which is **N**orth **A**tlantic **T**reaty **O**rganization .

active voice   Verb structure where the subject and the object of the sentence remain subject and object, in contrast with passive voice. Example: "I drove the car" is active voice; while "The car was driven by me" is passive voice.

adjective   A part of the speech that describes a noun, e.g. "the **gray** car." Unlike determiners, adjectives are non-grammatical words. In Spanish, the adjective goes after the noun "*el carro **gris**"* (= "the gray car"). This also defines a function within the sentence, so a group of words together can work as an adjective, e.g: "the **never-ending** story".

adverb   A part of the speech that describes a verb, an adjective or another adverb, e.g. "I drive **slowly**," "This is **very** intense." "I drive **very slowly.**"

article   A type of determiner. They are the words: "the," "a," and "an".

auxiliary verb A verb used to form compound tenses. An example in both
Spanish and English is the verb *haber* = to have, as in: "*Había ido
allí*' = "I had gone there," where "to have" does not posses an
actual meaning. It is used only to create the verb structure. In
English, other auxiliary verbs are: to be, to go, to do; e.g. "I **am
going** to study," "**Do** you work there?".

clause The grammatical structure with one verb (single verb, compound
verb or verbal periphrasis). Subordinate clauses cannot exist
independently, and they must be linked to the principal clause. For
example, the sentence: "If you wanted, I would go," has two
clauses: "If you wanted" and "I would go" .

cognate A word that is similar to other words of the same meaning in
another language. For example "Philosophy" in English with
"*Filosofía*" in Spanish.

conditional Verb tense that passes information on something possible due to a
condition: "I **would sing** in the theater, if I were famous." =
"*Cantaría en el teatro si fuera famoso*".

(to) conjugate To provide the six forms of a verb representing different persons
in a certain tense. To conjugate "to be" in the present is to say: "I
am, you are, he/she/it is, we are, you are, and they are".

conjugation Categorization of verbs of Latin origin corresponding to certain
schedule of endings. In Spanish, there are three conjugations:
verbs that end with AR, like *estudiar* (= to study), also called
verbs of the first conjugation; verbs that end with ER, like *poseer*
(= to posses), also called verbs of the second conjugation; and
verbs that end with IR, like *distribuir* (= to distribute), also called
verbs of the third conjugation.

conjunction A part of the speech that links nouns and verbs (like in "Francisco
and John," or "They studied **and** worked together"), or that link
clauses (like in "I will work unless you say something." A set of
words can work as a conjunction, e.g. "I will go **even if** you say
no."

consonant Speech sound pronounced by modifying the sound using lips,
teeth, tongue, etc., in contrast with the vowels. Consonant sound
represent the letters: b, c ,d, f, etc.

determiner | A part of the speech that describes a noun. Unlike adjectives, determiners are grammatical words. In both Spanish and English, determiners precede the noun, e.g. "**the** car," "**an** airplane," "**some** people." This also defines a function within the sentence; so, a group of words together can work as an determiner, e.g. "**some of those** people."

dieresis | In Spanish, a pair of dots over the letter "u" (ü*)* indicating that the letter "u" is not silent. For example *pingüino* (= penguin).

direct object | The part of the sentence over which the verb acts, e.g. "I saw **him**," or "I saw **a cat on the roof**."

false cognate | A word that is similar to another word in another language but has a different meaning. For example, the English word "assist" looks similar to the Spanish word "*asistir*;" however "*asistir*" means "to attend".

false friend | See false cognate (*Chapter 8 How to Learn Words Efficiently*).

feminine | Grammatical gender in contrast with masculine. In Spanish all nouns have grammatical gender, including objects. For example, *planta* (= plant) is feminine.

future | Verb tense that passes information about the future ("Tomorrow I **will sing** in the theater" = "*Mañana cantaré en el teatro.*")

gerund | Verb form incorporating -ING. It is a form of the verb that has no tense and no person. It can be used in English as a noun ("**Working** here is difficult.") or as a verb form ("I am **working**.") In Spanish, the equivalent -ANDO, -IENDO can only be used as a verb form.

grammatical word | Word that does not have an absolute meaning. In general they are prepositions (of, in, etc.), conjunctions (and, or, but, etc.), pronouns (I, you, me, etc.), determiners (the, a, some, etc.), some adverbs (very), and the auxiliary verbs.

imperative | Verb tense that expresses a command (**Sing!** = *¡Canta!*). The verbal moods comprise the indicative, the subjunctive and the imperative. The imperative mood only has one tense: the imperative tense itself .

imperfect past | One of the two past tenses of the indicative mood, together with the preterite. In English it is commonly translated by the continuous past tense ("Yesterday **I was singing**, when I saw him), in contrast with the preterite ("Yesterday I sang in that theater") .

indicative | Set of verb tenses that pass definite information, in contrast with subjunctive tenses, which reflect emotion, doubt, or possibilities ("He is going to school today"). (Indicative, subjunctive and imperative are called the verbal moods). In Spanish, the tenses of the indicative mood are: the present, the preterite, the imperfect past, the future, and the conditional.

indirect cognate | Word that is not directly translatable (recognizable) from one language to another, but which has similar derivative words. For example "*tener*" = "to have;" which are linked by other words like "*contener*" = to contain, or "*sostener*" (= to sustain).

indirect object | The part of the sentence that receives the action of the direct object, e.g. "He said that to **me**," or "He said that to **all senators**." Generally, you need a direct object in order to have an indirect object. In some constructions the direct object is understood.

infinitive | A form of the verb that has no tense and no person, and that can function as a noun of the clause, e.g. "**To sing** is hard." In Spanish all infinitives end with AR, ER or IR.

interjection | A part of the speech that can form a clause by itself, e.g. "hi."

irregular verb | Verb that doesn't follow a set of rules, in contrast with regular verbs. For example, the verb "to brake" is regular, and "to break" is irregular, since, in the past tense at least, "to break" has an irregularity: "I broke."

irregularity | A form of a verb in a person and a tense that does not follow the rules. If a verb has at least one irregularity, it is called "irregular." In English, the verb "to send," for example, is irregular. The form "sent" is an irregularity of the past tense (it is not "sended") .

local word | Word that is used in specific areas to the exclusion of other areas. For example on the East Coast, they use the term "thru way" and "package store" instead of "freeway" and "liquor store" respectively (*Chapter 8 How to Learn Words Efficiently*).

masculine	Grammatical gender in contrast with feminine. In Spanish, all nouns have grammatical gender, including objects. For example, *carro* (= car) is masculine.
non-grammatical word	Word with actual meaning. In general, they are: nouns (table, house etc.), adjectives (red, blue, etc.), and verbs (to sing, to eat, etc.)
noun	A part of the speech that identifies an entity, and that can work as subject of the clause. A noun can be: a person, animal, plant or object, tangible or intangible, e.g. "patience."
passive voice	Verb structure where the object of the sentence become the subject and vice versa, in contrast with active voice. For example: "I drove the car" is active voice; "The car was driven by me" is passive voice.
past participle	A form of the verb that has no tense and no person. It can be used as an adjective ("I am **tired**") or as a verb form ("I have **tired** my students in the gym"). In Spanish, past participles end with: -ADO, -IDO.
past subjunctive	Tense that expresses emotion, doubt or possibility in the past. Typically it doesn't exist in English. You can only find it in rare cases like: "If I were a rich man, I'd go," where "were" is used instead of "was." An example in Spanish is: "*Esperaba que él cantara más.*" = "I expected that he **sang** more."
periphrasis	Verb structure with more than one verb functioning as one. For example, the sentence "I **stopped smoking** years ago." has two verbs in tandem; and "They **are going** to **continue trying**," has four verbs in tandem.
person	Each of the possible forms of the verb as defined by its subject. Persons are: I /we (first person); you (second person); he/she/it/they (third person).
plural	Grammatical number that means more than one, in contrast with singular (which means one). For example the word "lions" is plural.
prefix	A construction at the beginning of the word that alters meaning, e.g. un-, dis-, pre- (*Chapter 8 How to Learn Words Efficiently*).

preposition   A part of the speech that introduces a noun clause, e.g. "to," "at," "in," and "on."

present indicative   Verb tense that passes information in the present. It has several uses: 1) it indicates a fact ("Two and two **equals** four"); 2) It shows a habitual action ("He **sings** everyday"). In Spanish, it has two extra uses: 3) it shows an instant action ("*¿Qué haces?* = "What are you doing?"), where English uses the continuous present tense; and 4) it shows an historic fact ("*Colon descubre America en 1492*" = "Columbus discovered America in 1492"), where English uses the past tense.

present subjunctive   Tense that expresses emotion, doubt or possibility in the present. Typically it doesn't exist in English. You can only find it in rare cases like: "I expect that he **sing** more" = "*Espero que él cante más,*" where "sing" is used instead of "sings."

preterite   One of the two past tenses of the indicative mood, together with the imperfect past. In English, it is commonly translated by the past tense ("Yesterday I **sang** in that theater"), in contrast with the imperfect past ("Yesterday I was singing when I saw him").

pronoun   A part of the speech that substitutes a noun in the third person. For example, "the man" can be substituted by "he," or "the persons" by "they." For example, "I told **him**" instead of "I told that man." The realm of the term pronoun is extended to other persons because of their similarities: I, me, mine, you, yours, we, us, ours.

reflexive verb   A type of verb that has an object that is the same as the subject, e.g. "He is going to dress himself."

regular verb   Verb that obeys a set of rules, in contrast with irregular verb. For example, the verb "to brake" ("I braked") is regular, and "to break" is irregular. In the past tense at least, "to break" has an irregularity: "I broke."

sentence   A grammatical structure that fully conveys meaning. It can have one or more clauses. A sentence must end with a period.

singular   Grammatical number that means one in quantity, in contrast with "plural," which means more than one. For example, the word "lion" is singular, "lions" is plural.

spanglish   Code switching between Spanish and English; an English word (original or altered) used in the Spanish speech, e.g. *"Tomaré la freeway"* (= I'll take the freeway), where "freeway" is not a Spanish word. In the sentence: *"Iré a la marketa"* (= I'll go to the market"), marketa is an alteration of the English word "market" with the typical Spanish suffix of the nouns: "a" (*Chapter 8 How to Learn Words Efficiently*).

stress   The emphasis in the intonation of a word. In Spanish, stress is always on one, and only one, syllable (specifically in one vowel of it). For example, the word "computer" has the stress on the second syllable "com-pu-ter."

subject   The part of the sentence (person or thing) that is or does something.

subjunctive   Set of verb forms that reflect emotion, doubt or possibilities. Typically it doesn't exist in English. In English you can only find it in sentences like: "If I **were** a rich man, I'd go," in contrast with indicative tenses, which pass definite information ("He studies everyday"). Generally only the subordinate clause of a two-clause sentence can have a subjunctive tense. In the example above, "I'd go" is the principal clause, and "If I were a rich man" is the subordinate clause. Indicative, subjunctive and imperative are called the verbal moods. In Spanish, the subjunctive mood comprises two tenses: the present subjunctive and the past subjunctive.

suffix   A construction at the end of the word that alters meaning: ing, ly, ness, age, etc. (*Chapter 8 How to Learn Words Efficiently*).

syllable   A division of a word into separate sounds. For example, the three syllables com-pu-ter form the word "computer." Letters form syllables; and, in turn, syllables form words (*Chapter 4 Syllable and Stress*).

verb   A part of the speech that represents an action, e.g. "sing," "be," "see."

verbs like "gustar"   A type of verb that has an object that functions as the subject. In the sentence "Fish revolts me." = "El pescado me revuelve." the real subject (who actually does the action) is "me;" however "me" functions as an object (since it is placed after the verb). Not the same as the passive voice, however. *"Gustar"* means "to like," and it is a common verb in Spanish that works this way (Notice that "to like" does not work the same way in English).

vocabulary   A set of words and their meaning (*Chapter 8 How to Learn Words Efficiently*).

vowel   Speech sound pronounced without obstacle (i.e. without using lips, tongue, teeth, etc.), in contrast with the consonants. Vowel sounds represent the letters: a, e, i, o, u, and occasionally "y."

Abbreviations & Symbols

e.g.   "Exampla gratia," Latin for "for example."

etc.   "Etcetera," Latin for "and the rest."

i.e.   "Id est," Latin for "this is."

i   In this book, "irregular verb."

ñ, Ñ   The only Spanish letter that is not part of the English alphabet. It can be seen in some English words with Spanish origin: piñata, jalapeño pepper, or el niño.

underlined letter   In this book, used to indicate e, e.g. comp<u>u</u>ter.

=   In this book, used to indicate "means" e.g. *carro* = car.

¡   Spanish symbol to begin an exclamation sentence.

¿   Spanish symbol to begin a question sentence.

→   In this book, "is converted to."

USING ENGLISH TO LEARN SPANISH

AUTHORS

Francisco de la Calle Bruquetas founded Bruquetas Publishing in 2009. A native of Madrid, Spain, Mr. De la Calle holds a M.S. from the *Universidad Politécnica de Madrid* in industrial engineering, and a M.A. from San José State University in Spanish. He has worked as an engineer, and has taught Spanish at university level. Mr. De la Calle is the co-author of the book series *Using English to Learn Spanish* as well as the author of a collection of fiction in Spanish.

Michelle de la Calle is a native born Californian. As a De Anza Nursing Program Graduate R.N. she joined the Peace Corps in Guatemala, where she taught basic hygiene and health to young rural children. She holds a B.S.N. from San José State University, and a Master's in Forensic Science from National University. Mrs. De la Calle, a Nurse Manager, has worked in the hospital setting for over ten years.

USING ENGLISH TO LEARN SPANISH
BOOKS OF THE SERIES

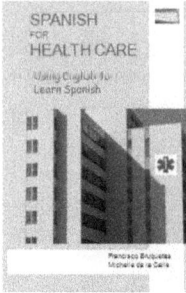

SPANISH FOR HEALTH CARE

Spanish for the Health Care is intended **for professionals** with no previous knowledge of Spanish. **The goal is to communicate with patients.** The book focuses on the dialogue to understand symptoms, and convey diagnostics and instructions.

The right way for professionals to learn Spanish is to learn the Spanish of the profession.

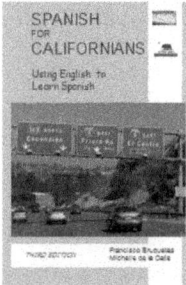

SPANISH FOR ENGINEERS

Spanish for the Engineers is intended **for professionals** with no previous knowledge of Spanish. **The goal is to communicate in your technical environment.** Each chapter focuses on one specialty, including construction, software, M&E engineering and project management.

The right way for professionals to learn Spanish is to learn the Spanish of the profession.

SPANISH FOR CALIFORNIANS

Spanish for Californians shows the Spanish of **Latin America and the U.S.** One of the twenty-two Academies that represent Spanish is in the U.S. The book teaches the common within the norm.

A textbook for beginners, and a reference data book for speakers. The easiest way to learn is by learning the simplest first.

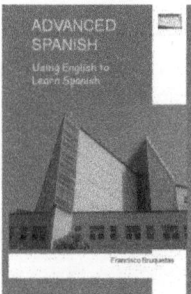

ADVANCED SPANISH

Advanced Spanish focuses on **those topics that are an obstacle for your fluent Spanish.** The textbook explains the subjects with many examples and comparisons to English.

Now that you can communicate, it is time to get to the point and perfect your Spanish.

www.ingramcontent.com/pod-product-compliance
Lightning Source LLC
Chambersburg PA
CBHW030932090426
42737CB00007B/393